LEWIS GRIZZARD

Don't Forget To Call Your Mama...

I Wish I Could Call Mine

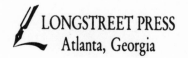

LONGSTREET PRESS
Atlanta, Georgia

Published by
LONGSTREET PRESS, INC.
2150 Newmarket Parkway
Suite 102
Marietta, Georgia 30067

Printed in the United States of America

1st printing 1991

Library of Congress Catalog Card Number 90-063904

ISBN 0-929264-93-2

This book was printed by Arcata Graphics Book Group,
Martinsburg, West Virginia. Cover printed by Mid-City
Lithographers, Lake Forest, Illinois. The text was set in ITC
Bookman Light by Typo-Repro Service, Inc., Atlanta, Georgia.
Book design by Jill Dible.

To my precious aunts,
Una and Jessie, my other mamas

Introduction

My mother was the third child of Charles Bunyon and Willie Word of Carroll County, Georgia. They named her Christine.

Her two sisters, Una and Jessie, called her "Cricket." Her two brothers, Johnny and Dorsey, called her "Teenie." Nearly three decades of first graders she taught knew her as "Miss Christine."

I called her Mama.

I have no earthly reason why. I could have called her Mother, of course. Ma and Mom were also available. I knew a kid who went with Mommy. He was a sissy.

Mama just came out of my mouth one day and stuck for the nearly forty-three years she and I had together. Mama died October 1, 1989, two days short of her seventy-seventh birthday.

The primary cause of her death was a disease called scleroderma, Latin for "dead skin." It is a rare disease for which there is no known cure. Mama suffered with it for more than years.

It attacked her esophagus. It caused the esophagus to lose some of its ability to move food down to the stomach. Mama's first symptoms were heartburn and indigestion. Then came frightening choking episodes.

Later her esophagus closed almost completely. Twice a month she had to undergo the torturous experience of swallowing a tube to reopen the esophagus.

What else happened was that Mama developed an eating disorder. She became *afraid* to eat. Food burned in her insides. Food caused her to choke. Food became her enemy.

In the initial stage of her disease and subsequent disorder—when she was still able to work and do the cooking for her husband, my stepfather—she simply put the food on the table for him and then took a plate for herself into the living room to eat alone.

She had to take small amounts and chew thoroughly. It could take her as long as 45 minutes to finish one plate. She didn't want anybody else to see her eating. She was embarrassed by the effort it took.

Slowly she began to reject food altogether. She stopped cooking. She didn't want to see food, much less eat it. My stepfather, H.B., began to cook for himself. Mama wouldn't even go into the kitchen anymore.

She lost weight. She lost her strength. The

family went on a crusade to get food down her. We begged her to eat. We pleaded. Mama's favorite food had always been fried shrimp. I brought loads of it from Atlanta restaurants home to little Moreland, Georgia, forty miles to the southwest where Mama lived near her sisters and brother.

She wouldn't eat the fried shrimp. I tried strawberry ice cream. That had been her favorite flavor. She refused that, too.

Her eating became birdlike. A spoonful of this. A little soup. H.B. bought a blender. Her diet became all liquids.

And Mama went to bed in the back bedroom. She took a disability retirement from teaching. H.B. had to quit his job. She had become his full-time responsibility.

Mama became, for all practical purposes, a recluse. When I visited her, I had to go into that back bedroom and pull a chair next to her bed.

H.B. would walk in and ask, "Will you eat some dinner for me?"

"I'm not hungry," she would reply.

"Mama, you've got to eat," I would say.

"I can't, son, I just can't," was always her response to me.

H.B. never gave up. He'd bring a plate to her anyway. A little helping of mashed potatoes run through the blender. Maybe some applesauce. Meat was out of the question.

One evening I sat next to her bed, coaxing her to eat. H.B. had put her pitiful little plate on a tray. I got an idea.

"Mama, do you remember what you used to do when I was a little boy and you fed me?" I asked her.

She didn't recall.

"Well, I do," I said. "I can remember like it was yesterday. You used to put me in your lap and take a spoonful of food and pretend the spoon was an airplane. You would fly the spoon around my head and make a noise like the plane's engine.

"Then you'd say, 'Okay, the plane is about to land. Open your mouth.' And then you would fly the spoon into my mouth. Do you remember that?"

She forced a little laugh and said, "Well, I guess I do."

"Okay, then," I continued. "Now, it's your turn."

I took a spoonful of food off her plate. I flew it around her. I made the sound of an airplane engine. The child, now the adult. The adult, now the child.

"Okay," I said, "the plane is about to land. Open your mouth."

She opened it slightly. I put the spoon between her lips. She took the food.

I got three or four more spoonfuls down her. Then she said, "Son, I'm tired of this game.

4

Let's quit."

Eventually Mama became non-ambulatory. She wouldn't eat and wouldn't get up out of that bed anymore. The last fifteen years of her life, the only times she left that bed and that house were to go to Humana Hospital in the county seat of Newnan, six miles north of Moreland.

The hospitalizations became more frequent and became lengthy. Her malnutrition and that bed began to cause painful and serious side effects. She developed circulation problems and bedsores. She would become dehydrated. So, off to the hospital for fluids. Maybe a week or two weeks.

Then back home and back to that bed again until another trip to the hospital was necessary. The last fifteen years of Mama's life, she was hospitalized at least a hundred times. The tops of her hands were permanently blue because of the number of IV's she had to endure.

Her limbs began to atrophy. Her feet became swollen and drawn. She developed painful arthritis in both her hands. They became swollen to twice their normal size.

At one point, Mama was brought to Atlanta and hospitalized. Doctors there examined her. Nothing could be done for the scleroderma. A psychiatrist was called in to see if he could help in getting her to eat. He failed.

5

So the vicious cycle continued. Month after month, year after year.

I saw her waste away. The robust, energetic mother who had raised me became a pitiful picture of agony and suffering.

H.B. never left her side. He administered her medicine. He bathed her. He clothed her. He came up with the best idea anybody, including the doctors, had during mother's last years.

He got her out of that back bedroom. He didn't get her out of bed, but he got her out of that dark place in the back and into the living room. He bought a hospital bed, moved the chair and table and lamp on one side of the living room, and put Mama's bed in that spot.

I think it kept her alive longer. Visitors used to go one at a time to that foreboding back bedroom. But in the living room, she could be around all her visitors at once. There was more of an opportunity to include her in conversations and family discussions.

The doctors think the scleroderma did reach Mama's brain in the last years of her life. She suffered periods of disorientation. Her memory suffered.

Occasionally she would speak out and ask, "Where is my mama?"

Someone would answer, "Your mama's dead. She's been gone a long time."

That would send her into a long period of silence. Once, after having her question answered, she cried. A few minutes later, she said, "I sure did love my mama."

But I think the living room and the opportunity to be back in the family circle certainly gave her more periods of lucidity.

There were times she would laugh. There were times she actually would initiate conversations. These are precious memories.

My mother's legacy has so many parts to it. There is the sadness and pain and suffering. But there is also a lesson in survival.

Despite Mama's self-enforced period of reclusion, despite the hospitalizations and agonies I could not conceive, she fought for her life.

"She has an incredible will to live," one of her doctors told me. "She has fought harder than any patient I have ever had."

Once, during a visit to her hospital bed, when she was listed in serious condition with all sorts of problems and complications, I stood above her as she slept.

Suddenly she opened her eyes and looked at me and said, "Lord, I hate to die."

But she came back that time and she kept coming back, and who can know just how many times she turned back an insistent death.

Mama. She walked into a headwind most of her life. But she survived. She endured. She overcame. Her accomplishments were against odds that would have brought so many of the rest of us to our knees.

Mama. I loved her so. She loved me more.

Mama. This is my tribute to her.

1

Mama married Daddy in 1942, and soon afterwards he was shipped out to Europe and World War II.

He came back in 1945, and I was born in October, 1946, in Fort Benning, Georgia, where he was stationed. The Army soon had us living in Tallahassee, and then on to Camp Chafee, Arkansas, and to Fort Myer, Virginia, Daddy's last stop before Korea.

Daddy survived a near massacre of his company by the Chinese. He hid under the stacks of dead who were his comrades and spent six weeks trying to get back to the U.S. lines. He was listed as missing in action for those six weeks.

Captain Lewis M. Grizzard, Sr., was a good soldier. He had landed at Normandy on D-Day. He had fought through France and on into Germany. He had won a Bronze Star for valor, a battlefield commission, and a Purple Heart.

But war can kill a man in more ways than one. Daddy couldn't handle much of anything after Korea. Alcohol. The Army. Money. He and my mother stopped sharing a bedroom a few months after he came home.

He drank too much. He cried all the time. He ran up huge telephone bills, calling drunk into the night. He ran away from the Army. He ran away from us. And one day Mama found herself in a house in Columbus, Georgia, her man gone for good, with bills she could never pay and with a little boy wondering what sort of demon had taken his daddy away and left his mother in tears.

The only place she knew to go was back to her parents. Charles Bunyon and Willie Word had moved to Moreland in Coweta County from the homeplace in Carroll County when he couldn't keep the farm going anymore. Their oldest daughter, Jessie, and her husband, Grover, had moved earlier from Carroll County to Moreland to work in the village knitting mill.

Mama Willie got a job in the hospital in Newnan taking care of new-borns. Daddy Bun helped out at the Atlanta and West Point Railroad station, became the janitor at the elementary school, and ran a little fruit stand on Highway 29 that went through Moreland.

He also was able to buy twelve acres of land in Moreland. He built Mama Willie a little white frame house on the land, which was across a dirt road called Camp Street from the Baptist Church.

Jessie and Grover then built a house next to Daddy Bun's and Mama Willie's on one portion of the land. Later, their youngest son, Dorsey, built his family a house on the same land.

On what was left of the plot, Daddy Bun planted corn, potatoes, okra, and tomatoes, and spring onions. Dorsey and Jessie's son, Scooter, helped with the planting and the plowing and the harvesting.

We moved to Moreland in the summer of 1953. There were four rooms and a bath in my grandparents house—a kitchen, a living room and two small bedrooms. The house was heated by a kerosene stove in the living room. There was an open back porch with two chairs and a swing for two on it.

Daddy Bun built himself a little shed to the back of the house. He kept his tools there. He stored his corn there. He planted strawberries and scuppernong vines behind the shed. He also planted fruit trees—apples, pears, plums, pomegranates and figs.

We also had a few chickens who produced fresh eggs every morning. Daddy Bun bought a little Briggs and Stratton garden tractor one year. Before he had plowed with a borrowed mule.

My grandmother and Aunt Jessie both loved flowers. Their yards were showplaces in the springtime. Between the house and my grandfather's shed was a weeping willow tree. On

Sunday afternoons, the family would gather under the tree to make homemade ice cream or cut a watermelon.

I had lived in cities and on large Army bases the first six years of my life. I'd never seen a mule. I'd never reached up and plucked a piece of fruit from a tree. I'd never been around that many country folk, and some of their ways were foreign to me at the outset of my life with my grandparents.

I didn't know some people still didn't have indoor toilet facilities. Several of the children I joined in the second grade at Moreland School still went to outhouses and bathed in water heated in a pot on the stove.

Some of the children in the second grade at Moreland came to school barefoot until Christmas, when they received shoes as gifts.

Some were out of school when cotton picking time came. I met sons and daughters of sawmillers, sharecroppers, dirt farmers, and mill hands.

By following my grandfather around, I learned new, amazing facts about things like guano, post hole diggers, garden snakes, .22 rifles, and how to put snuff on a yellow jacket sting to ease the pain and remove the stinger.

I learned what cotton poison smelled like, how to pour sorghum syrup onto your plate and then sop it up with a biscuit, and the number of each train that came up and down the

A&WP tracks through Moreland.

I missed my Daddy and would never stop missing him. But Daddy Bun did his best to fill in.

Mama Willie read to me from the Bible, cooked three grand meals a day, and gave me my first responsibility. I was in charge of emptying the slop bucket. The slop bucket sat in the kitchen. There was no garbage disposal, of course, so every disposable thing left over in the kitchen went into the slop bucket. Egg shells. Coffee grounds. Chicken bones. Peelings. *Slop.*

I had to take the bucket out twice a day and pour the slop into a hole that had been dug near my grandfather's shed. I emptied the slop and then covered it up with dirt to keep down the smell.

Mama got a job teaching first grade in Senoia, Georgia, a few miles out of Moreland, in the fall of 1953. She was paid $120 a month. She bought a used 1948 Chevrolet to go back and forth to school.

I'd had my own bedroom in our house in Columbus. In Moreland, there were only two beds. My grandparents slept in one. My mother and I slept in the other, which brings up my mother's hair.

Mama's hair, before it turned gray, was black. In pictures I saw of her as a young woman, she wore it cut short with curls to the left and right of her forehead.

My mother's hair nearly killed her in 1948. When we were living in Arkansas—I was two and retell this from later conversations—Mama began to lose her hair. She became quite alarmed, of course (she was in her mid-thirties at the time), and finally sought medical advice.

Doctors found she had an infection on her scalp. More of her hair fell out and the infection grew worse. Treatments were not working.

When local doctors felt they had no other solutions, they recommended that mother be sent to Walter Reed Hospital in Washington. It was her first trip aboard an airplane and she often talked of the fear she felt.

"They had me strapped down in a bed," she recalled. "There was no way to see out of the plane. I knew when we landed and I knew when we took off again. We must have made ten stops between Arkansas and Washington.

"I was sick and frightened out of my mind. I told God if he would get me down out of that thing, I'd never fly again."

Mama's plane landed safely. She never flew again.

My father and I took a train to Washington a week later when doctors reported her situation was worsening. Nobody could ascertain what had caused the scalp infection, and it raged on. I can vaguely remember my father taking me to visit Mama in Walter Reed. I can still see her completely bald, her scalp covered with ravaged flesh.

Mother's sister, Una, had come to Washington to take care of me during the crisis. She said I often told playmates that I had two mothers.

"I didn't think Cricket was going to make it," Una would tell me later.

And my mother told this story of a dream she had in the hospital.

"I dreamed I was standing at a beautiful lake," she began. "You were playing down near the water. There were many flowers and birds. Suddenly, I looked across the lake and I saw your daddy's mother, Miss Genie.

"She called to me and said, 'Don't come across. Your little boy is going to need you.'"

Mama, said the doctors, made a miracle recovery.

Daddy got a transfer to Fort Myer, and mother came home to the married officers' barracks. She wore bandages on her head for weeks.

Some of her hair eventually came back, but she had a permanent bald spot on the back of her head. As hair from other parts of her head grew longer, she was able to comb it back to cover the bald spot. But Mama never got over the sensitivity she felt about her hair. She constantly complained about it.

"Una," she would say to her sister, "I just

can't go out with my hair like this."

No trip to the beauty parlor ever satisfied her.

"Now, that looks nice, Cricket," Una would say to her after she returned.

"That woman just ruined my hair," Mama would reply.

Mama's hair became my prime symbol of security. I was a frightened little boy. If my Daddy could go away, why couldn't my mother?

The kerosene stove in the living room at my grandparents' barely heated the kitchen and the living room during the winter. So the bedrooms and the adjoining bath were closed off. Hitting those sheets at bedtime was like diving into a cold pond. Some nights, Mama even heated bricks on the kerosene stove and put them at the foot of our bed to warm us under the piles of homemade quilts.

I began holding my mother's hair when we slept together in my grandparents' home. I would cling to it all night. As long as I had her hair in my hand, she could not leave me.

I clutched her hair. I twirled it in my fingers. I pulled at it. I must have kept her awake many nights, but she never complained.

A few years ago, I received a letter from a female reader who said she had a problem. How familiar it sounded. She said she was divorced and worked days and went to school nights. She said she had a five-year-old boy who slept with her.

"He just won't keep his hands out of my hair at night," she explained. "I know he's frightened, but it's gotten to the point I can't sleep. I need to sleep to be able to get through the long day ahead of me. When I take his hand from my hair, he starts crying and won't stop until I let him put it back. I've tried to get him to sleep in a bed by himself, but he just won't do it. What can I do?"

I understood the woman's problem, but I also understood her son's. I wrote a column about the letter and told the woman, "One night all too soon, you will be lying in your bed, wishing you still had that little boy next to you, out of harm's way, with his hand in your hair. Enjoy it while you still can."

Mama married my stepfather, H.B. Atkinson, when I was ten. The ceremony was at the Moreland Methodist Church.

My grandfather was a deeply religious man, a hardshell Baptist. He believed in the practice of washing feet, which had been standard in his home church. He did not believe in a minister having notes. He thought the word should come from above, directly to the man behind the pulpit. Daddy Bun quit going to church in Moreland because they didn't wash feet and the preachers had been to seminaries.

"You don't learn to preach in no school," he said.

When he refused to enter the church for the marriage, I was drafted. I gave the bride away.

H.B. and I had a rough time of it in the first years of his marriage to Mama. The primary reason was that he took my place in Mama's bed, and I was banished to the couch in the living room. No more hair to hold onto.

I cried, pouted, held my breath, saw faces in the window, banged on Mama's bedroom door, pitched various fits, and cursed the day Mama brought that man home to live.

That lasted until I was about twelve and H.B. and Mama built a house between Dorsey's and Jessie's, not far from Daddy Bun's and Mama Willie's in a spot cleared out from a portion of the cornfield.

I got my own bedroom and a radio from Sears Roebuck. After that, I spent my nights searching for clear channel sports broadcasts and was weaned off Mama's hair.

I picked up the practice again when I married. All three of my ex-wives have awakened many mornings with their hair in tangled knots. Currently I am living with a dog. He won't sleep with me.

2

Mama could have solved the current federal deficit problem. All the government would have had to do was hand over all its money to her and say, "We're spending more than we're taking in. Could you help us?"

Indeed, she could have. She would have cut the government's needs down to a bare minimum. No new interstate construction for awhile. She would have cut out all that $63 for a screwdriver business by the defense department and figured out a way to get a volume deal with a hardware store at $1.50 a screwdriver. Lawmakers, bureaucrats, and others on the federal payroll would have had to make do on less.

"We don't need anymore rocket ships to outer space," Mama would have told NASA officials. "They've already messed up the weather as it is."

My mother's frugality knew no bounds. There were several reasons for that.

First, she had been raised by parents of

modest means who believed that spending unwisely was as big a sin as working on Sunday and drinking.

Second, she lived through the Depression. It had made a remarkable impression on her.

"We made it because we grew our own food, and the family worked daylight to dark, and not a penny earned ever left for anything we could do without, and you'd be surprised at all the things people think they can't live without but can."

She mentioned, as items that fell into that category, a great many things that I thought were necessary for any semblance of a full life. There was candy, and milk shakes at Lee King's drug store in Newnan, and a new baseball, and money for movies and Cokes and popcorn.

As I got older, that list changed a bit. Replacements included a motor scooter, madras shirts, money to buy my girlfriend an ensemble of Evening in Paris perfume and powder for her birthday, a trip to Daytona Beach with older friends during the summer, and the Great Gold Cup Socks Controversy, which needs to be explained further and is the source of why, even today, I avoid socks whenever possible.

The dress for a pre-teen boy in the early fifties was quite simple: a white T-shirt, blue jeans, tennis shoes (which cost around five bucks, instead of what it costs to buy a Buick as it does today) and white socks.

Mama bought my socks at Judson Smith's warehouse south of Moreland. Judson sold cut-rate clothes, better known as "seconds," at a very cheap price.

Mama bought my white socks in a bundle, six pairs for less than a dollar. To be sure, Judson's socks were a little thin and tended to lose some of their elasticity at some point during their first wearing, but who could argue with six pairs of socks, of any description, for less than a dollar. I was quite happy with my socks.

Then my cousin Jimmy came to visit. Jimmy was the son of my Uncle Johnny, Mama's oldest brother. Uncle Johnny was a doctor. Jimmy took one look at my socks and laughed.

"Where did you get those stupid looking socks?" he asked.

"What's wrong with my socks?" I asked him back.

"They're too thin," he explained. "You need athletic socks like I'm wearing."

Cousin Jimmy showed me his socks. They were white, like mine, but they were, indeed, much thicker and made of an obvious better grade of material.

"How long have you had those socks?" I asked him.

"A year," he said. And their elasticity seemed completely intact.

"What do socks like that cost?" was my next question.

"Dollar a pair," he said.

I was astounded. *A dollar a pair.* It cost a dime to go to the Alamo Theatre in Newnan. A Big Orange belly washer, as they were called, was only a nickel.

After Jimmy left, I told Mama that my Judson's socks wouldn't do anymore. I needed athletic socks.

"What do they cost?" Mama asked me.

"Dollar a pair," I answered.

After being revived, she said, "I've never heard of such a thing."

The following Christmas, there was a pair of white athletic socks in my stocking. I wore them to school five days a week, to the envy of my friends, and then Mama washed them on the weekend.

After the eighth grade, Moreland children were bused six miles to Newnan High School. Newnan was a prosperous community. Cotton money. Old money. Doctors. Lawyers. Bankers. The Newnan boys laughed at my white socks.

"You don't wear those anymore," they said. "You need to get some Gold Cups."

Gold Cup socks, it turned out, came in different colors. The idea was to match your Gold Cups with your shirt.

"How much are Gold Cups?" I asked a New-nan classmate.

"Two dollars a pair," he answered.

Same story. Mama's eyes rolled back in her head and she lost consciousness temporarily. But for Christmas, there were two pairs of Gold Cups in my stocking—a light blue pair to go with my blue shirt and a yellow pair to go with my yellow shirt.

I made it all the way through high school on those two pairs of socks. Then I went off to the University of Georgia.

My freshman roommate, George Cobb, Jr., from the great metropolis of Greenville, South Carolina, saw my Gold Cups and laughed at them.

"You don't wear socks like that in college," he explained. "You need dark, over-the-calf socks."

Third verse: "How much do they cost?"

"Four dollars a pair."

That was it. I loved my mother, and I wasn't about to put her through the sock shock again. So in the autumn of 1964, I simply quit wearing socks. Sure, my feet got cold during the winter, but I endured the pain and actually started a trend that continues today.

Many Southern males no longer wear socks. Check them out the next time you're at a cocktail party at any Southern country club. Even Guccis with no socks. I've actually made a career of not wearing socks. Albert Einstein didn't wear socks, either, you can look it up.

Mama's frugality stemmed from two other sources. When Daddy left, she basically was penniless. I think of her in that Scarlett O'Hara scene where she says something like, "I'll never go hungry again." Mama would never again be caught in such a financial emergency. She would do without, scrimp and save, and an emergency would never find her empty of pocket again.

The main reason Mama was so frugal with money, however, was that she had determined that, no matter what, her child would get a college education.

I was an original Baby-Boomer, the first crop in '46. The catch phrase for Baby Boomer parents was, "I want you to have it better than I did."

"When the time comes for college," Mama would say, "I'll have the money."

Lord, the ends to which she went.

When the old '48 Chevy quit, Mama had to buy another car. She had fretted about it for months. Such a major financial commitment to buy another car. She drove the '48 until it just lay down one day, turned over on its roof and died, belching smoke and spitting oil.

Somebody told Mama she could get a great deal on a new '55 Chevy south of Moreland in

Manchester, Georgia. So we went there in Uncle Dorsey's truck, and Mama haggled with the salesman until he was willing to make any sort of deal just to get her off the lot.

Mama bought a new 1955 Chevy. It was green. A rather God-awful shade, I might add. And we are speaking generic car here. Mama didn't want any chrome. Mama didn't want any whitewall tires. If Mama could have gotten by without a manifold, she'd have done it.

When the salesman asked, "Would you like for us to put in a radio?" Mama was adamant.

"Radio?" she asked incredulously. "What on earth do I need a radio in a car for?"

I don't think Mama bought one stitch of new clothes for herself while I was in high school. As much as she fretted over her hair, she might have made one visit to the beauty parlor a year.

Additionally, she was perhaps the greatest bargain shopper in history. She never bought a morsel of food without making certain it wasn't being sold cheaper at another grocery store.

She bought cut-rate ice "milk" instead of ice cream, and only about one carton of that a month. She got a deal on day-old bread at a local bakery. I never saw a bar of soap with writing on it until I was nearly grown. Mama always bought some plain off-brand, and until it had become almost microscopic due to repeated washing, she wouldn't buy another bar.

To squeeze a tube of the cheapest toothpaste anywhere other than the very bottom was an offense punishable by a severe tongue-lashing. Then there was the deal about toilet paper.

I will attempt to be as careful as I can here not to overstep the bounds of good taste by being overly descriptive, but the toilet-paper deal was a large part of my life as a child. Even as a small boy, I liked to use a lot of toilet paper. I had a special thing about toilet paper. I suppose it stemmed from all those stories older relatives told about the days when corn cobs were the forerunners of Charmin.

Also, I had visited homes of some of our rural relatives who still had outhouses, with a lot of wasps flying around, and the only available material for the final stage of a bowel movement was pages from an old Sears Roebuck catalog, which were quite harsh and lacked absorbent qualities.

I hated such situations and always tried to find a page without human forms pictured upon it out of respect. I normally searched for pages advertising garden hoses or kitchen appliances.

So when I was at home, I relished the fact that we had indoor plumbing and toilet paper, so gentle. I tended to use it in abundance. Consequently, we often violated Mama's one-roll-a-week rule, despite the fact that there were four of us living in my grandparents house and three after she married H.B. and we moved into our own house.

"You're using too much toilet paper, young man," Mama would say to me.

I didn't want to talk about such a sensitive subject, even with my own mother. I would mutter or babble incoherently.

I might have avoided notice of my inability to use toilet paper in moderation, but I tended to use so much that I often clogged the toilet, which would send mother into a rage as well.

Mama put me on a strict toilet paper budget. "I just can't afford your toilet paper habit," she said.

I was allowed to roll off four individual toilet paper sheets twice. That was it. My own mother even demonstrated to me how to use one side of the paper ration, then turn it over to the other side and use it again.

Perhaps part of Mama's concern with the toilet paper usage had to do not only with saving money but also with her plan to instill in me the desire for higher education. Often she spoke about the fact that I could not expect to be a financial success in life unless I earned a college degree.

As I folded my little handful of toilet paper over to the other side to save money for my education, I often said to myself, "If I ever do

27

get out of college and become a financial success, I'll use all the damn toilet paper I want."

I did get out of college and I did become somewhat of a financial success, and I have used so much toilet paper at various sittings that I have single-handedly kept several plumbing concerns in business.

Despite Mama's careful watch over the money, there were a few financial crises that came about. H.B. was laid off from his job with a local gas company for a time, and we went on the highest state of alert during that period. I ate a lot of bologna sandwiches.

Still, Mama managed to save. She kept pennies and dimes in a jar. She kept shoe boxes of small bills in the far reaches of closets. She quit smoking. Not for her health, but because she could save if she dropped her quarter-a-day habit.

All for me. All for my education.

I was a good student in high school. To have made poor grades and risked college rejection would have hurt Mama more than if I had joined a gang that stole hubcaps and wore greasy, ducktail haircuts.

The day my acceptance from the University of Georgia came, Mama cried. The day I left home for Athens, she cried again.

After my freshman year, I began to work full-time at an Athens newspaper. I later won a scholarship. I was able to pay a lot of my college expenses on my own. But even then, Mama always worried if I had enough money.

"Have enough for books?" she would ask when I called home.

"You sure you can pay this quarter's tuition?" she would ask another time.

I worked in college mainly because I loved my chosen profession and figured out early that practical experience was the best teacher of the skills I sought. But Mama paid for my start, and if I had not chosen to work, she would have paid for it all.

In some ways, I think she even felt disappointed that I provided some of my own college costs.

I married at nineteen. It was a year later before my bride and I were able to take a honeymoon. Mama paid for our four-day cruise to the Bahamas. She insisted. I still felt guilty. All that going without and now she was sending me to the Bahamas.

Mama gave me the down payment on our first house. She insisted again. Mama said, "Whatever I got, son, it's yours."

"Spend something on yourself," I would often tell her before she became bed-ridden and could have splurged a little on her own pleasures.

But she never did. And when I got into a position to begin giving back, it was too late.

3

I wanted to give Mama a lot of things. I felt I owed her for what she had done to get me educated and out into the world making a few dollars. And I loved her, too. And when I was a child, buying Mama a gift was the way I used to get out of trouble.

Until I was about ten, Mama tied my shoelaces each morning. I've never been very good with my hands, and I simply couldn't get the hang of tying my laces. (I was also a failure as a Boy Scout, but that's another story.)

So Mama tied my laces, but I was hard to please. I wanted them tied tightly, but not too tight, and anything short of perfect usually resulted in what was known as "pitching a fit," which basically consisted of crying and whining and stomping.

Whenever I would do something like that, say the morning of a school day, Mama would say, "Young man, I don't have time to deal with you now, but I'm going to wear the filling out of you this afternoon."

What a horrible thing. I had to sit in school all day worrying about getting my filling worn out when I got home.

So I devised a plan. I got a quarter a week allowance. I usually had at least fifteen cents in my pocket at any given time. On my way home to my thrashing, I would stop by Cureton and Cole's store near Moreland School and buy myself a Coke and a bar of candy, which came to a dime. Then I'd buy Mama a nickel's worth of something like fig newtons.

When Mama came home from school, I would run and jump into her arms and say, "Mama, I love you so much. Look at what I bought you out of my allowance." This naturally would put her in a forgiving mood, and I wouldn't get my punishment. Not only that, I'd also usually get to eat the fig newtons.

Once Mama got sick, it became harder and harder to buy her anything. She wanted a larger television in the living room because she couldn't see the old one. So I bought her a larger television.

Mama wouldn't let me put an air conditioner in the house, but she would take a ceiling fan in the living room.

I bought her a portable phone to make it easier for her to talk to callers from her living room bed.

Her circulation became very poor. She suffered from arthritis. I had the bright idea to rebuild the little bathroom of her house and put in a Jacuzzi. I thought it might help her circulation and ease some of her pain.

That suggestion went like this:

"How about a Jacuzzi?"

"A what?"

"You'd love it. A Jacuzzi is a big tub, and you fill it with hot water and there are all these jets shooting out water and you sit in there and it's very relaxing. It would be great for your arthritis."

"I never heard of such a thing."

"What we could do is knock out a wall and extend the bathroom."

"I don't want a bunch of carpenters sawing and hammering and tracking mud into the house. Don't get me a bacuzzi."

"Jacuzzi."

"However you say it, I don't want one."

So what else can you do for your invalid mother? I'd have given her a trip anywhere in the world. Obviously that wasn't possible. Even if Mama had been healthy, she wouldn't have flown. I would have built her a new house, but she would have said, "There's nothing wrong with the house I'm in."

What I did was buy Mama a lot of gowns. I bought silk ones and cotton ones. I bought them plain. I bought them in bright colors. I bought them with floral patterns.

"Oh, son," she would reply when I opened a

box and pulled out a new gown and handed it to her in her bed, "this sure is a pretty gown, but you didn't need to spend the money on me."

We had only one real Christmas together, my mother, my father and I. Only one Christmas when we were actually in our own house with coffee and cake left out for Santa, with an excited five-year-old awakening to a pair of plastic cowboy pistols, a straw hat, and an autographed picture of Hopalong Cassidy.

My first Christmas I was only a couple of months old, and that doesn't count. Then we were traveling around for a couple of years. The Army does that to you. Then there was Korea. And then we had that one Christmas together before whatever demons my father brought back from Korea sent him to roaming for good.

That one and only Christmas together, my father had duty until noon on Christmas eve. I waited for him at the screen door, sitting and staring until that blue Hudson— "The Blue Goose," as my father called it—pulled into the driveway. I ran out and jumped into his arms.

"Ready for Santa?" he asked.

"I've been ready since August," I shouted.

But before we could settle in for our Christmas, my father had to take care of a problem. He had found this family—the man out of work, in need of a shave and a haircut, and his wife crying because her babies were hungry. My father, whatever else he was, was a giving man. He couldn't stand to have when others didn't.

"They're flat on their butts and it's Christmas," I remember him saying to my mother. "Nobody deserves that."

So he somehow found a barber willing to leave home on Christmas eve, and he took the old man in for a shave and a haircut. Then he bought the family groceries. Sacks and sacks of groceries. He bought toys for the kids, of which there was a house full. The poor are often fruitful.

We didn't leave them until dusk. The old man and the woman thanked us, and the kids watched us with wondering eyes.

As we drove away in "The Blue Goose," my father broke down and cried. My mother cried, too. I cried because they were crying.

We all slept together that night and cried ourselves to sleep. Next morning, I had my pistols and my hat and my picture of Hopalong Cassidy.

Maybe the three of us had only one real Christmas together—my father had left by the time the next one rolled around—but it was a Christmas a man can carry around for a lifetime.

Each year at Christmas, with my father long

since in his grave, I thank God that one is mine to remember.

Mama was never big on Christmas after that. I think she liked Christmas okay, but even before she got sick, she tried to keep our Christmas celebrations with H.B. in Moreland to a minimum.

That usually started with an early-December pronouncement that went, "I don't think we'll have a big tree this year."

We *never* had a big tree. We started with a small tree and worked down, and finally Mama bought an artificial Christmas tree that sat on the living room coffee table. It was more of a Christmas plant than a tree.

One Christmas, H.B. decided that since all we had was a table tree, he would string lights across the front of the house.

Mama was against that idea from the start. "I don't know why you'd waste money on lights," she told H.B. "We're so far off the road nobody is going to see them in the first place, and we've already got a tree."

H.B. would not be denied, and I was in his camp. There was no opportunity for me to throw tinsel on a tree, spray it with that snowy-looking substance that came in an aerosol can, or get on a chair to put the star on top of the tree. So stringing lights across the front of the house seemed a grand yule adventure to me.

We went out there one cold December evening and carefully tacked several strings of Christmas lights onto the front of the house. Mama remained inside worrying about how much the lights had cost.

The big moment came. The lights were up. H.B. sent me into the house to turn on the juice for the lights. I flicked the switch. There was a hideous popping sound. Not only did the Christmas lights not come on, but every light inside the house went off in a massive blowing of fuses.

We had to eat by candlelight. The next morning, H.B. went out and took the lights down from the front of the house.

The following year, he suggested we put lights on a tree in the front yard. Mama said, "Don't you go near that tree with Christmas lights."

Mama's first-graders gave her a poinsettia that year. We made do with that and the toy tree she brought out from the back of some distant closet from the Christmas before.

This is not to say we didn't have happy Christmases. We just didn't fall victim to any excesses. And most years, my Christmas wishes came true.

I got an air rifle when I was ten, despite the eternal parental fear that any child with an air rifle would shoot out at least one eye within an hour of taking possession of it.

When I asked for an air rifle, Mama said,

"Didn't you hear about the little boy in Hogansville? He got an air rifle and he was running with it and fell down and the rifle went off and shot out one of his eyes."

It was the old "little boy in Hogansville" trick. Mama saw me running through the yard with a sharp stick once. She said, "Don't run with that stick. A little boy in Hogansville was running with a stick and he fell down and put out one of his eyes."

Another time, I was going swimming with some friends at a local farm pond. "You be careful," Mama said. "A little boy in Hogansville was swimming in a pond and he stepped off into a deep hole and drowned."

No wonder. The kid was blind.

Still, Mama got me the air rifle and I managed not to shoot out an eye. I did shoot a bird once, however. I think it was a sparrow. The bird fell out of the tree and writhed in agony on the ground. It proceeded to die right in front of my eyes.

I was just playing around with my air rifle. I didn't actually mean to kill the bird. I picked up the dead bird, got a shovel from Daddy Bun's shed and dug a hole near the scuppernong vines and buried it.

I was heartbroken and sick and scared. Later, I told Mama what I had done and asked her, "Do you think I can still get into heaven?"

"God forgives," she assured me.

I sort of lost interest in my air rifle after that incident. The following year I wanted a radio. Mama ordered me one from Sears Roebuck. Another year, I asked for a bat, a ball and a glove. I got those as well.

There were only two Christmases I failed to get what was at the top of my list.

When I was twelve, I wanted a Flexy Racer. A Flexy Racer, the fore-runner of the skateboard, was a wondrous instrument.

What you did was lie down stomach first on a Flexy Racer, which had four sets of wheels underneath it. There was a handle on each side you could turn in order to move right or left. You got on your Flexy Racer in front of the Methodist Church on the Moreland square and aimed it toward the railroad tracks, located down the paved hill.

My friend John Cureton had a Flexy Racer. He allowed me a turn or two down the hill. I was the wind.

When I asked Mama for a Flexy Racer for Christmas, she had me describe it to her. I mentioned the part about being the wind, soaring down the hill from the church towards the railroad tracks. I shouldn't have done that.

"What if you couldn't stop and a train was coming?" she asked.

"This hasn't got anything to do with a little boy from Hogansville, does it?" I asked Mama. I didn't get a Flexy Racer.

Lewis Grizzard

When I was fourteen, I asked for a motor scooter. Dudley Stamps, my friend, had a motor scooter. I wanted my own desperately.

"You're not getting a motor scooter," Mama said.

"Why?" I asked.

"They're too dangerous," she answered.

"But Dudley's got one," I countered.

"And Dudley will probably fall off that thing and put out one of his eyes, too," she said.

I got a desk for my bedroom and some underwear and pajamas that year.

When Mama became sick, I think she actually dreaded Christmas. She couldn't get out of the house to shop for presents for the family, and that made her feel guilty. Sometime around Thanksgiving, she would look up from her bed and say to me, "Son, don't get me anything for Christmas this year. I can't get to town to get you anything."

"I don't expect that, Mama," I would reply, "but I want to get you something."

"I just don't want to be any trouble, son."

"It's no trouble, Mama. I want to get you something. What do you need?"

"I can't think of a thing."

"What about some new gowns?"

"I'll never wear the ones you've already given me."

"Need any warm house shoes? I know your feet get cold."

"I've already got some."

"How about a warm sweater?"

"You gave me one for my birthday. Why don't you take the money and buy yourself something. Do you have a warm coat?"

"Three of them."

"What about a hat?"

"I don't wear hats, Mama."

"Well, how do you keep your head warm?"

"My head doesn't get cold."

"Have you got enough cover for your bed?"

"Plenty, Mama. What if I just surprise you with something?"

"If that's what you want to do. I just don't want to put you to any trouble."

"No trouble."

One year I gave her a down blanket with ducks on it. She liked the ducks.

Another Christmas I gave her a cassette player and some gospel and country tapes, Mama's kind of music. And the last Christmas she was alive, I couldn't think of anything else to buy her, so I brought another gown, a pretty blue one.

"That's the prettiest gown I've ever seen," Mama had said. Nine months later, we buried her in it.

Rarely does anyone give up a parent or a mate or a brother or sister or a friend without regret. I have my own when it comes to Mama.

41

I am ashamed of it but will tell of it. Perhaps others can avoid the same mistake.

What Mama always wanted most, what cost the least and meant the most, was a simple phone call. I didn't call Mama enough. I called her, but not enough. I tried to remember to call at least twice a week, but I'd be travelling or get caught up in some project, and I'd just plain forget.

It was difficult talking to Mama on the phone the last several years of her life. Once I said, "Mama, how are you?" and she answered, "I guess I'm doing *pretty* good." It was hard to get any lengthy dialogue going after that.

There were times I even felt like it was hard on Mama to get a telephone call. She had lost some of her hearing and had to ask me to repeat most everything I said. She often would put the receiver at her mouth and would complain to H.B., "I can't hear Lewis."

He would turn it around for her. What she always was interested to hear was when I was coming to visit her.

"Mama," I'd say, "I'll be down to see you a week from Monday."

"A week from when, son?"

"Monday, Mama. Anything you need me to bring you?"

"I can't think of a thing."

"Anything you need to talk to me about?"

"Well, I guess not."

"I love you, Mama."

"I love you, too, Sugar."

"Let me talk to H.B. before I go."

"Okay."

"Bye, Mama."

"Bye, son."

That was about it for the last years of her life.

Still, when I would visit Mama, she would always tell me as I left, "Don't forget to call me. I just like hearing your voice."

H.B. chastised me at times when I'd go a week or two without calling. "She always seems to sleep better after she hears from you," he said.

Yeah, I regret not calling her more. There's some guilt that will probably remain with me. It's such a simple little thing to do. Call your Mama. Even if you talk for just thirty seconds, she enjoys it. She might even *live* for it.

A true story:

I was at Point Clear, Alabama, speaking to a group of South Central Bell executives. At dinner, some of us were swapping stories about the Bear. Alabama's late, great football coach, Bear Bryant.

A gentleman who handled the advertising account for South Central Bell was recalling when Bryant was hired to do commercials for his South Central Bell account.

"What the Bear was supposed to say at the

end of the commercial was, 'Call yo' Mama,' as only he could say it.

"But we were shooting, and he just ad-libbed a line. He said, 'Call yo' mama.' And then he added. 'I wish I could call mine.'

"We never would have asked him to do something like that, but it worked out perfectly."

Another of the Bell executives carried the story further.

"Soon after the commercial began running," he said, "my secretary came in and said there was a customer on the line that just had to talk to me. I was pretty busy, but I figured if she was being that persistent, I should talk to her.

"When I got her on the phone, she asked, 'Are you the one responsible for the Bear Bryant commercial on television?'

"I sort of wanted to ask her how she liked it before I took responsibility for it. But I said, 'Is there any problem?'

"She said, 'Gracious, no. But I just wanted to tell you a story: My husband and I were sitting watching television the other night, and we saw that commercial for the first time. We were very moved when Coach Bryant said, "I wish I could call mine."

"'I got right up and called my own mother, and we chatted for a few minutes. I forget to call her sometimes, and she gets worried about me.

"'My husband's mother is still alive, too. I

asked him why didn't he call his mother, and he went straight to the phone and called her. They must have talked for forty-five minutes. I'd never known him to stay on the line with anybody forty-five minutes, much less his mother.

"'They talked about old times, and he told her how much he loved her.'

"I said to the woman," the executive continued, "that her story was really heartwarming and I appreciated her passing it on.

"She said, 'You haven't heard all the story yet. Less than an hour after my husband hung up from talking to his mother, she died. He never would have had that conversation with his mother if it hadn't been for Coach Bryant's commercial.'"

I don't have to hit you over the head with the message, do I?

4

I never had Mama as a teacher. I missed her by two years. I attended first grade at Rosemont Elementary school in Columbus. Daddy was stationed at nearby Fort Benning.

I was in Moreland School for the second grade. What I recall most vividly about my first day at Moreland was that a couple of ruffians, the brothers Garfield, made a small bomb out of gunpowder and set it off on a window ledge in the second grade room as our teacher, Mrs. Bowers, was welcoming us to her class.

The bomb blew out several windows, sent Mrs. Bowers screaming to the principal's office, and I, along with several other students, wet my pants.

One of the Garfields was ten, having failed first grade twice, and the other one was nine. It took him only two years to get out of first grade.

The principal suspended the Garfields from school for a week, which is what they wanted and why they set off the bomb in the first

place. More about the Garfields and their ter-
roristic activities later.

Mama's first job teaching after Daddy split
was the first grade position at Senoia School,
ten miles west of Moreland.

The following year, however, the first grade
job came open in Moreland and Mama filled it.
The school was in walking distance of my
grandparents' house. That was a lot easier on
Mama. She would teach first grade there for
two more decades.

Having your own mother as a member of
your school's faculty had a couple of advan-
tages. One, I could go by her room on my way
home each afternoon and ask for a few coins
to spend on treats at Cureton and Cole's store.

A Coke was a nickel. So was a Zagnut candy
bar. There were two benches outside the store.
My friends and I would drink our Cokes and
eat our candy and speak of the day's affairs
and hope we could finish both before one of
the Garfield brothers showed up and took
them away from us.

Another advantage had to do with recess. We
took one in the morning and one in the afternoon. Each class would take part in some sort
of physical activity, accompanied by their
teacher. The fact that my mother was on the
playground made it less likely that one of the
Garfields, or any other number of boys who
could beat me up, would do so. I even had a

distinct advantage in a boys' playground game called Squirrel. Whoever invented Squirrel was a sick person. And simple-minded. You ran up and grabbed somebody in the gonads, squeezed and said, "Squirrel! Grab the nuts and run!"

The problem with Squirrel was that you couldn't simply say, "Thanks, but I'd rather not play today." If a Squirrel game broke out on the playground, you were in it.

One day, somebody started Squirrel. I had managed to avoid a few earlier attempts at my crotch with some artful dodging and even showed several flashes of flanker speed. It's amazing how much faster you can run if you're fleeing an individual who wants to inflict serious pain by squeezing your testicles.

I was never, ever a pursuer in a Squirrel game. First, I thought the game was a little odd. Even then I knew there was something, well, not exactly right about grabbing at another boy's crotch. I wasn't even aware of the possibilities as they applied to girls at that point.

Also, I didn't want to introduce the revenge element in the game. So I get somebody at Squirrel. It would make them just that more determined to get me back.

On this particular day, I was fairly sure the recess bell would save me from any direct hits, what with my speed and footwork. But then two of my classmates came at me. Could I avoid them both?

Then I heard one of them say, "Aw, leave him alone. He'll go over to where the first graders are and cry to his Mama and she'll send us to the principal."

I was happily saved from the horrid fate that likely had awaited me, but that also brings up one of the disadvantages of having your mother teach at your school.

I sort of got a reputation as a "Mama's boy" amongst some of the older boys, a horrid fate in its own right.

First, there was the business about the fact that my father wasn't around. Divorce was a rare thing in those days.

"Where's your daddy?" was a question I got often.

Mama had said to tell them that he had been a good soldier but that he was sick.

Then the word got out that I was still sleeping with my mother, and then somebody else leaked the fact that I was eight years old and my mother was still tying my shoes. (Hey, I did finally learn when I was nine. I never could do much with mechanical things.)

"Mama's boys" were supposed to be weak, easily frightened, and spoiled. The fact is that I was all three and still am to a degree. But I wasn't what else was supposed to go along with being a Mama's boy—a sissy.

I was no sissy. The quickest way to figure out
whether or not a boy was a sissy was to watch
him throw a baseball. If he threw it with too
much wrist and not enough extension of the
arm, that was all you needed. The child was a
sissy. Other sissy characteristics were wearing
rubber overshoes on a rainy day, not wearing
blue jeans and white T-shirt or white socks
with tennis shoes, not belonging to the Boy
Scouts, and failing to know the participants in
the last World Series.

Well, none of that applied to me. I had a
wicked curve ball by the time I was ten. I once
struck out all eighteen batters in a six-inning
church-sponsored boys baseball league. By the
time I was twelve, I had learned to scuff the
ball so it would curve even more and how to
grab my own crotch on occasion and spit
through my teeth like Reggie Jackson.

I never wore rubber overshoes. I didn't even
own a pair. I wore the uniform, and I can still
tell you the starting lineup of the 1956
Brooklyn Dodgers, the victims of Yankee
pitcher Don Larsen's perfect game in the World
Series that year.

But we were talking about having your
mother teaching in your school. The teachers
expected more of you, of course. They figured
any child of a teacher was naturally smarter
than any child of, say, a welder or a truck
driver. That's not always true, but it was

accepted as fact.

I got a lot of, "Your mother certainly wouldn't be happy if she knew you turned in such sloppy work."

There was also the matter of classroom conduct. Alice McTavish, the biggest girl in my class and one of the biggest in five counties, sat behind me in the third grade. Alice was an aggressive child. She could also beat up most of the boys her age, including me.

One morning during arithmetic class, she began thumping my ears from behind. At first I decided not to retaliate and risk angering Alice, who would then proceed to thrash me, mother on the playground at recess or not.

But the ear thumping got to me after a while, so I turned around in my desk and tried to bonk Alice on the head with my fist.

Unfortunately, the teacher, who hadn't seen the provoking ear thumping episodes, saw my swing, which had missed, by the way. Alice caught it with a forearm.

"I cannot believe you, the son of a teacher," she admonished me, "would attempt to hit a girl right in the middle of class."

I tried to explain, but the teacher wouldn't listen.

"I'm going to talk this over with your mother at faculty meeting this afternoon," she went on.

Great.

At the dinner table that evening, Mama said

to me, "I've never been so embarrassed in my entire life as I was when your teacher told the entire faculty what you did in class today."

"Mama," I began, "Alice isn't like other girls. She's bigger than this house."

"Probably just a gland disorder," Mama said, "and you had no business trying to hit her."

I tried to get in a few more words regarding how my swing, which never had a chance of landing, was provoked. Mama wouldn't hear of it and said that if she ever heard of me doing anything like that again, my punishment would be swift and harsh.

A few weeks later, however, Alice broke Alvin Bates' nose when he asked her if she had won any prizes at the hog show at the county fair, and Mama said, "I guess Alice is a rather stout girl for her age."

Having a mother around to protect you on the playground certainly is a benefit, but there was one occasion when I had to beg her not to report a rather painful incident to the principal.

I had managed to stay unmarked by the Garfield Brothers, other than a few punches to my arms and the day the elder, Frankie, got me in a headlock and rammed my head into the tether-ball pole, but Frankie had been just kidding around. When Frankie was serious about hurting someone, he did not let them go until they were bleeding, exhibiting large knots and bruises, and groveling around on the ground screaming pitifully for mercy.

In the fifth grade, I finally got mine. I had ridden my bike to school. Afterward, I was riding down the path that led away from the school on my way to Cureton and Cole's store.

It was a very narrow path, and at the end of it was a deep ditch that forced a hard left turn. A seventh grader named Billy Gaines was in front of me, walking quite slowly. There wasn't room to pass him on my bike, and besides, something like that might be deemed a lack of respect for somebody two years older than me and Billy Gaines might have taken offense and belted me.

The problem arose when Frankie Garfield walked up behind me and my bicycle. "Get that damn bicycle out of my way. I'm in a hurry," Frankie demanded.

I wanted to get my damn bicycle out of his way, but Billy Gaines was in my way.

I decided if Billy Gaines beat me up for passing him, it would be better than Frankie Garfield beating me up for not getting out of his damn way.

So I took Billy on his left and began pedaling as fast as I could. Unfortunately, I apparently had not acted as quickly as Frankie had wanted me to.

He ran behind me and my bicycle. When I got to the end of the path and the deep ditch in front of it, I had to slow down to make the hard left-hand turn.

The moment I slowed, Frankie lifted up the back of my bicycle and flipped it, with me astride it, into the deep ditch.

At mid-flip, I came off my bicycle seat and landed nose first in the ditch. My bicycle then landed on top of me. Frankie walked into the ditch after me, but after seeing my nose bleeding and my face scratched and a giant knot on my forehead, he figured the job was done and proceeded on to the store to forcibly detach other children from their Cokes and candy bars.

My bicycle wasn't damaged nearly as much as I was. Except for a small dent in the front fender, it came out of the experience quite well. I rode my bike home as fast as I could.

My mother wasn't home from school yet, my grandmother was working in her flowers, and my grandfather was plowing.

I went into the bathroom and took a survey of the damage to my face and head. I looked like I'd been in an ax fight and finished fourth.

I tried to wash away as much mud and blood as I could. I even tried to press the knot on my head flat. That didn't work.

My fear was this: Mama sees me in this condition and wants to know under what circumstances I had received such ghastly wounds.

I rarely lied to Mama. Actually, I always lied

when I thought telling the truth wasn't a good idea. But Mama usually unveiled the truth eventually.

She finally would force it out of me that I had fallen victim to a Garfield, and the following day at school she would tell the principal. The principal would then call Frankie into his office. He would ask the other male on the faculty to come into the office, too. Even a grown man didn't want to have to deal with even just one Garfield alone.

He would then suspend Frankie from school for a week. That would delight Frankie, but he would also be angry that I had ratted on him to my mother, so the first opportunity he got, he would pummel me further. On top of that, he would probably tell his brother, David (a.k.a. "Killer"), and he would also take his turn at bruising my person.

I went outside and avoided Mama until dinner time.

"What happened to your face?" she asked. "And that knot. How did you get that knot on your head?"

"Bicycle accident," I said.

"You weren't trying to ride and not hold to the handle bars were you? A little boy in Hogansville was doing that, fell off his bike and a stick stuck in his eye and now he's half-blind."

"I was riding down the path after school and

I thought I was farther away from the ditch than I really was, and so I went too far before I tried to turn left and I rode my bike into the ditch and I fell on my nose and head."

Not bad.

"It was one of those Garfields, wasn't it?" Mother said.

How does she always know these things?

Still, I stuck to my story.

"It wasn't a Garfield, Mama," I said.

"Are you sure?"

"Sure I'm sure."

What gave me away when I lied to Mama? Did I do something funny with my mouth? Was I unable to look her directly in the eyes when I answered one of her interrogatives?

"Did one of those boys hit you?" she asked.

"No ma'am," I said. Well, he didn't *hit* me. At that point, I was hoping she didn't use the verbs "flip" or "push" or "shove" next.

"You've been down that path hundreds of times," she went on. "I just don't think you'd drive your bicycle directly into that ditch. Now, you tell me what really happened this instant."

I told her.

"I'll see Frankie Garfield in the principal's office in the morning," she said. "I'm tired of those boys bullying you children around. They're too old to be with you kids anyway."

Just as I thought.

"Mama," I started, "please don't tell Mr. Killingsworth (our principal). He'll call Frankie in and then Frankie will beat me up again, this time worse."

"I have to report something like this to the principal. You're hurt badly. He could have broken some bones."

"He will if you tell the principal," I said.

Mama turned thoughtful.

"Okay," she said, "I won't tell the principal, but I'm going to have a talk with Frankie myself."

"He'll still kill me," I said.

Mama wasn't to be denied. She took me into the bathroom and put something that burned terribly on the cuts on my face, and she put a cold wash cloth on my knot and suggested it would be gone by morning.

"I'll have four more by tomorrow afternoon," I said.

"No, you won't," she said.

The fact that I was still alive by the time school ended surprised me greatly. I figured I'd be dead by lunchtime anyway. I had spent the morning daydreaming about what my funeral would be like. There would be lots of crying, of course, and they'd probably sing "Precious Memories." It was a terrible thing to think about, dying. I wondered if there would be baseball in heaven. I was certain that's where I would go. The only Commandment I'd breached at that point in my life, besides killing that bird with my air rifle, was that I had coveted the electric train Bobby Entrekin had received for Christmas. It blew real smoke. Mine didn't.

That didn't seem like much of a sin, really, when you considered that Bobby Entrekin also had his own football helmet and I didn't. I figured God probably would even overlook that one little transgression as he flipped through my list of good deeds, like dutifully taking out the slop bucket and actually making an attempt on cutting back on the toilet paper I used.

When school was over, I didn't even ride my bicycle down the path. I passed up the afternoon trip to the store, too. I took another route home and went into the bedroom and got under the bed. If the Garfields came looking for me at home, maybe they wouldn't think to look under the bed.

Forty-five minutes after I got home, I heard Mama come in the door. She walked in the bedroom and asked for me.

"I'm under the bed, Mama," I said.

"Well, come out from under there," she said. "Frankie Garfield isn't going to hurt you."

Mama called the sheriff. That's what had to have happened. She had called the sheriff and he had come to get Frankie, as well as his brother, and had taken them to jail. I would be safe until they were released. I began to wonder how long a sentence you got for throwing somebody and his bicycle into a ditch.

Mama said to come into the living room and sit down. She had something to tell me.

"Before I talked to Frankie," she said, "I pulled his records. Do you know he doesn't live with his daddy or his mama?"

I didn't know that.

"His aunt is raising both those children alone. His daddy is dead and they don't know where his mama is. I talked to the other teachers, and they said before his mama left, she used to beat those boys. They simply haven't known much love in their lives, and that's why they have turned out the way they have.

"They haven't had any spending money for Cokes and candy like you have. They haven't been taken to Sunday School or church. I doubt they've even been in a picture show in their entire lives. All they know is that they have to fight for everything they get. I really feel sorry for them."

This wasn't exactly what I had expected.

"Do you know what I did?" Mama asked.

I had the feeling that whatever she did hadn't involved the sheriff.

"I had Frankie come down to my room during recess, and I asked him if he would help me put up the children's blocks and crayons and clay from the morning. I told him if he did,

I'd give him a quarter and he and his brother could go to the store after school and spend it on whatever they wanted.

"He was as nice and co-operative as he could be. So I told him if he would come back and help me tomorrow, I'd take him and his brother and you to the show in Newnan Saturday. I'd never seen a boy smile quite that much. He ran and got his brother and brought him back to the room.

"'Miss Christine says she's going to take us to the picture show Saturday. Tell him, Miss Christine. Tell him.'

"I said, 'I told Frankie if he would help me in the room tomorrow, I'd take you both and Lewis to the show in Newnan. Do you like that?'

"He said, just as polite as he could, 'Yes ma'am.' Those were the two happiest boys I've ever seen leave that room."

Obviously, the ditch incident of the previous day had damaged my hearing. Me going to the picture show in Newnan with the Garfields? Me, alone with the Garfields, in a darkened theatre sitting through a Flash Gordon serial, a cartoon and a Randolph Scott feature? I wouldn't make it to the first horse chase scene.

I protested. "I'm not going," I said.

"Yes, you are," Mama said. "The Bible tells us, 'Love thy enemies.'"

"The Bible also says, 'Thou shalt not kill.'"

"Those boys just need some love and attention," Mama replied.

Saturday morning, we drove to where the Garfield brothers lived to pick them up. Where they lived was what had formerly been a house. At this point, it might have been classified as a shelter but obviously not a very good one. There were windows broken out on one side. One Garfield brother probably had thrown the other through the window. Or they had been practicing at home for bombing the school window.

Mama honked the horn on the '55 Chevy. A woman appeared on the front porch of the house. She was in a tattered house coat. Her hair was multi-directional.

"Won't you come in, Miss Christine?" the woman said to Mama. "I'm Frankie and David's aunt, Pearl."

Mama got out of her car. I stayed put. As Mama approached the porch, Frankie and David came out of the house. They seemed to be uncharacteristically well-scrubbed.

I heard the Garfield's Aunt Pearl say to Mama, "I shore do appreciate you doin' this for the boys. I ain't got no car to take'em no where."

Mama said, "Frankie worked real hard for me last week at school, and I know David will help me, too. Little boys like to go to the picture show."

Frankie and David got into the back seat of Mama's car. They were wearing old clothes, but they were clean and fairly wrinkle-free. Both had their hair combed. I'd never seen anything like that on a Garfield before. Even I could sense their anticipation of the adventure to Newnan and the picture show.

As we drove away from the house, Mama said, "Son, Frankie's got something he wants to say to you."

I turned around. Frankie turned his eyes downward. I also sensed a certain embarrassment on his part, almost a shyness. Was this the same Frankie Garfield, the Mengele of the playground? Frankie mumbled something I couldn't understand.

"Speak up," Mama said to him.

Still unable to meet my eyes, he said, "I'm sorry I threw you and your bicycle in the ditch."

I couldn't believe what I was hearing. Frankie Garfield apologizing to me? He hadn't even used the modifier "damn" when he referred to my bicycle.

"And what else Frankie?" Mama asked.

"I promise not to hurt anybody at school again," he said.

My God. A miracle. Dillinger goes straight. Atilla the Hun agrees to stop raping and pillaging.

"What do you say, son?" Mama asked me.

What I wanted to say was, "Hitler promised a lot of stuff, too." But I didn't. As a matter of fact, I was too stunned to say anything.

Mama finally said, "Tell Frankie you appreciate his apology."

"I appreciate your apology," I said to the front window. I was afraid to turn around and look at Frankie. I was afraid I would see him with his tongue stuck out at me, or see him doing the old slit-the-throat sign. I would believe all this when the Garfields could go an entire week without inflicting physical harm.

"You're not going to be rough on the boys at school either, are you, David?" Mama asked.

"Yes ma'am." said David. "I mean, no ma'am."

We rode on to Newnan in silence. What if this were nothing more than a clever ruse? What if the Garfields, once they got into the movie, decided to do something to me? Like hit me and take away my popcorn and Coke. What if they decided to attack the entire audience? What if they had brought a gunpowder bomb with then?

Mama stopped the car in front of the Alamo theatre. She gave each of us a quarter. It cost a dime to get into the movie. That left fifteen cents for a nickel Coke, nickel bag of popcorn, and some nickel candy. I looked at Mama. My eyes said to her, "Don't make me get out of this car."

"Go ahead," she said. "Everything will be okay."

What the Garfields did was ignore me. They were so mesmerized by the fact that they actually were at the picture show with a Coke, popcorn, and candy in their hands that they were not interested in killing or maiming anyone.

Flash Gordon ray-gunned half the universe in the serial. There was a Woody Woodpecker cartoon. Randolph Scott saved the ranch again in the feature.

Mama was parked on the curb when the three of us walked out. Frankie and David immediately began to recount the celluloid adventures they had seen on the screen.

When we pulled into their driveway back in Moreland, they got out of the car. David walked into the house. Frankie came to Mama's side of the car and said, "Miss Christine, do you need me to help you Monday?"

"I'll see you at school and let you know," she said. "Now, go tell your Aunt Pearl about the show."

He turned and ran toward his house. Mama watched until he disappeared into the shack. She smiled and then we drove away.

As far as I know, the Garfields never bothered anybody very much after that. And the three of us went back to the picture show a few more times.

The Garfields and I never became good buddies or anything like that. But Mama's kindness toward them obviously had had a profound effect. They always were at Miss Christine's beck and call when she needed them in the first grade room. They cleaned her blackboard and took the erasers out and dusted them. They watered the plants she had in her room and found a special pleasure in feeding the fish Mama had in a small aquarium.

After the eighth grade, we were all bussed to Newnan High School. David was sixteen his freshman year, so he quit school and somebody said he joined the Navy. I never saw him again.

Frankie didn't come back to school after his sophomore year. His Aunt Pearl died and he got a job at a welding plant in Newnan. I came home one weekend from college and Mama said Frankie had been killed in an auto accident. He and a friend had been drinking and they ran head-on into a freight truck.

"I didn't hear about it until a week after it happened," Mama said. "The county had to bury him."

Mama had that thing some teachers develop, the idea that her students were her children, too. Often when I visited her in the hospital, a nurse would come into her room and introduce herself to me and say, "Your Mama taught me in the first grade."

I must admit that I did have an educational advantage because my mother was a teacher, especially when it came to grammar. My mother was on constant grammar patrol at home.

Ain't was forbidden. So were double negatives. Put the two together and it was hell to pay, as in, "I ain't got no more homework to do."

"You *have* no more homework to do," Mama would correct me.

"That's what I said," I once replied.

Mama made me go out in the yard and pull weeds out of her flowers.

Words like *his'n* (his) and *her'n* (hers) I picked up at school. Also *are* (over *are*, instead of *there*), *cher* (here), *rat* (as in *rat cher*), not to mention the usage of a personal pronoun when it wasn't needed, as in "Mama, *she* went to town last night."

Those were all forbidden to me. So was, "Mama, where's the milk at?"

Her response was, "Behind that 'at.'"

"What do you mean, Mama?" I'd ask.

"Never end a sentence with a preposition," she would explain. "It's simply, 'Where is the milk?'"

I thought I had it.

"Tell me again the rule on prepositions," Mama said.

"Never use a preposition to end a sentence with," I replied.

Back to the weeds.

I have no idea how many first graders Mama taught during her career. Over the years, however, I've received a great many letters that began, "Your mother, Miss Christine, taught me in the first grade. . . ."

A nurse who was with Mama when she was pronounced dead at the hospital had been a student of hers.

I've often thought about first grade teachers. Most of us don't have the patience to teach children that young. Mama often said she spent the first six weeks of each year teaching half her class to ask permission to go to the bathroom instead of wetting their pants.

First grade teachers, I've come to believe, may be the most important teacher a person will have in his or her educational experience.

Reading and writing are the basis of all learning. First grade teachers teach that. Imagine being able to take a six-year-old mind and teach it to write words and sentences and give it the precious ability to read.

As for me, Mama taught me that an education was necessary for a fuller life. She taught me an appreciation of the language. She taught a love of words, of how they should be used and how they can fill a creative soul with a passion and lead it to a life's work.

I'm proud of my Mama, my teacher. On her tombstone we put "Miss Christine."

5

I was married and out of college when Mama's condition made it impossible for her to cook anymore. It was the greatest of ironies that a woman who loved good food and was so accomplished at preparing it would suffer a disease that made food her enemy. But I had seventeen years of full-time eating at her table, for which I will be eternally grateful.

One of the greatest compliments I can give to her cooking is that my mother never—not once—opened a can of those make-believe biscuits. Jerry Clower, one of my heroes, has always referred to those horrid things as "whomp biscuits," that coming from the fact that to open a can, the instructions say to hit it against the side of a table. "Whomp!"

"One of the saddest things," Jerry once said, "is the sound of them whomp biscuits being opened in more and more houses these days. Whomp! Another poor man is being denied homemade biscuits. No wonder the divorce rate is so high."

Mama made her biscuits from scratch, the same as her mother had done. They were soft as angel hair. When Mama and Daddy were living together, he called Mama's biscuits "cathead biscuits," as in, "Great God, Christine, what mahvelous cathead biscuits."

I asked him one day, "Daddy, why do you call 'em cathead biscuits?"

"Just look at one of these things," he said, holding up a biscuit. "They're as big as a cat's head."

There are a lot of things you can do with a good, homemade biscuit. The simplest maneuver is simply to slip a pat of butter into a piping hot biscuit, give it a second or two to melt, and then bite, chew and swallow a piece of culinary heaven.

I picked up this from my grandmother: Slice open the biscuit, put in the butter and then add a little brown sugar. The result is a sweet buttery, delight.

You can also put syrup on a biscuit. And then there's gravy, which further enhances the taste of a homemade biscuit.

Basically, there are two kinds of gravies that go so well with biscuits, and my mother made both of them.

There's milk gravy. I have no idea how Mama made it, but it was brown and thick. I have also heard this called "sawmill" gravy, but I know not of its origin.

Then there's "red-eye" gravy, which normally is made from the grease left in the pan after frying country ham. It's thinner than milk gravy and has a reddish tint, but it can pull a biscuit up a notch itself.

I cannot discuss Mama's biscuits without also discussing her eggs and the fine art of the sop.

First, allow me to admit openly and without shame that my mother spoiled me in many ways, especially when it came to feeding me, a fact that worked its way into helping dissolve a couple of subsequent marriages.

There was the way Mama fried an egg. When Mama fried an egg, and you broke the yellow with your knife or fork, it did not run willy-nilly across your plate. As a matter of fact, Mama's yellow didn't run at all. It *crawled*.

Mama fried her eggs *over medium well*. Over easy or over medium makes the yellow too runny, and I could never stand a bunch of thin, runny yellow stuff on my plate.

Over well, of course, turns the yellow into a solid mass, quite disturbing to one who seeks perfection in his fried eggs.

But *over medium well* is a masterpiece, and rarely in my adulthood have I been able to get my eggs cooked the way Mama cooked them.

And to "sopping" for a moment. Mama usually cooked me two fried eggs. After I had

71

finished the solid parts, some crawling yellow would be left on my plate.

I'd reach for another biscuit. I'd pull apart a chunk and run it through the yellow left on my plate. That was "sopping." You can sop syrup as well as gravy off your plate with a biscuit. The only humorous line I know about sopping is I heard a man say once, "I'm so broke I couldn't afford syrup if it went to a penny a sop."

Mama, of course, had other specialties besides biscuits and eggs. Let us begin with her fried chicken.

It was our normal after-church Sunday fare. Fried chicken with rice gravy and fresh vegetables from the family garden. Green beans (cooked for an hour with a little ham thrown in for flavor), fresh tomatoes, boiled new potatoes, creamed corn (that wasn't sweet like every damn serving of creamed corn I get today), squash, and maybe some spring onions from my grandfather's onion patch near the Baptist church cemetery. Mama would cook biscuits or some of her equally-as-impressive cornbread with that. Sometimes she'd even cook both.

But back to her chicken. I don't like runny eggs and I don't like fried chicken that has been fried to a serious crisp.

Mama fried her chicken in a big black skillet on top of her stove. And when it was served, it was, by-God, *done*. Don't give me no chicken, if you will pardon the grammatical license, that's got any juices left. Fried chicken is not supposed to be juicy, like they often serve it in a restaurant.

Mama's crust was perfectly browned, but the meat inside was dry. I can eat a steak with a little juice, but if you've ever smelled live, wet chicken, you would know why a cooked dead one should be void of anything that will flow downhill.

I liked white meat. Mama always saved the breast for me. H.B. never complained, but I often wondered if he were muttering to himself, "Why does he get the breast everytime and here I am with a wing and a back?"

Mama cooked dinner six nights a week. She took Sunday night off. But that was never a problem. She always cooked enough chicken for Sunday lunch that there would be several pieces left over for Sunday night.

Here's something else about chicken as well as biscuits: They're both pretty good cold. Around seven on Sunday nights (when "The Ed Sullivan Show" started off slowly with an opera singer or seals doing tricks), I'd go to the kitchen and search out the leftover chicken and biscuits. I would have eaten all the white meat for lunch, but there is absolutely nothing wrong with a good leg and a cold biscuit.

Mama's country fried steak took my breath

for years. She also could do wonders with a baked hen and dressing or with a roast or a ham.

But I must tell of my favorite meal Mama served me during my childhood and adolescence.

She would buy canned corned beef. It came in a squatty little can and was very inexpensive. Mama would open the corned beef, put it in her pan, toss in a little butter, and then fry it, also to a crisp.

With that she would serve white beans. (These are also known as "northern beans," but nothing that good can be northern, so I do not hold with that name.)

Also she would serve me French fries. Not French fries out of some box. Not *frozen* French fries, but French fries she had carved from a couple of potatoes with her very own hands.

Mama's French fries always had a nice outside crust but remained a little gooshey (if that is a word) on the inside.

I would get hot, buttered cornbread with that, along with some green onions and lots of her ice tea. It was a glorious concoction. I had a name for it—corned beef à la Christine.

I mentioned earlier about Mama's spoiling me and the effect it had on my subsequent married lives, currently standing at three.

My first wife was also from Moreland and

thought nothing of frying me up some corned beef and adding the aforementioned side dishes. My second wife came from rural South Carolina. She was not quite the cook my first wife was, but this can be explained by the fact that she was much younger than my first wife and didn't like country music.

But my third wife, Kathy—the one who wrote a book about me and later told the *New York Times* that I was basically a "doo-doo pot"—grew up in Atlanta. She came from a wealthy family. They had servants and maids. Besides all that, Kathy was a runner. She even ran the Boston Marathon. So she was into a health thing and had an aversion to anything fried.

It wasn't that Kathy was a bad cook. Quite the opposite. She could prepare the best tenderloin I ever ate. She also made great spaghetti. And I had begun eating my eggs scrambled by that time anyway, having finally realized that no other person on earth could prepare my eggs like Mama did.

We'd been married about a month when my wife asked me, "What would you like for dinner?"

I said, "How about some fried corned beef, white beans, hand-cut French fries, and cornbread?"

"Fried what?" she asked

"Corned beef," I said. "It comes in a squat little can at the grocery store. You take it out of the can and put it in a frying pan and add a little butter."

"My God," she said.

"What's the matter?" I asked.

"I've married a man who eats Spam."

"It's not Spam," I said. "It's corned beef that just happens to come in a can."

"I'm not cooking any Spam in this house," she replied.

I continued to argue, but I never got my fried corned beef and we got a divorce two years later.

Kathy was further perplexed because I preferred white bread over wheat, ordered my steak well done, refused to eat anything that even resembled broccoli and once tried to order a cheeseburger at Maxim's in Paris.

My mother's cooking, then, has had an effect on my adult life, and in more ways than causing me marital strife.

There's the ice tea problem. Mama's tea was sweetened, but she used saccharine. I have no idea why. I got used to Mama's tea, of course, but when I left her home I was confronted with tea I had to sweeten myself out of a jar of sugar.

I could never again recreate the taste of my mother's tea. So I quit drinking sweet tea altogether and, although I still drink ice tea by gallons, I am very partial to unsweetened. As a matter of fact, I avoid eating with friends who serve sweetened tea. Once I ordered tea in a restaurant and a man came out with tea in a can. I barely avoided throwing up on his shoes.

My mother's cooking was pure down-home Southern. I took her table for granted as a boy, but now I am on a constant search for food of that sort.

I despise fancy food. I've been to restaurants where they served the green beans damn near raw and cooked the tomatoes. I don't like sauces; I like gravy. And as a man said to his wife in a movie I saw once, "Don't serve me any 'ini' food." I'm like that. I don't want any linguini, and I especially don't want any zucchini.

I despise any kind of chicken that isn't fried—it's an insult to my heritage—and I've tasted cornbread that was sweet and suggested a pox upon the heretic who cooked it.

I used to eat a little Chinese food until a guy told me the Chinese sometimes cook cats. I can abide Mexican food once a month. I don't eat anything French, except fries, and I ordered something off a German menu once and they brought me a weenie that was a yard long stuck in the middle of a little hard roll. The only thing I like Italian is a soup they serve in Italian restaurants. They call it *pasta rigomortisini* or something like that, but it's basically a bunch of beans cooked with ham hock.

I went to Greece once and they tried to serve me squid and octopus. Remember in one of those old movies based on Jules Verne books when that giant squid or octopus swallowed an entire ship? I don't eat anything with tentacles that tries to eat a ship.

English food is rarely fit to eat. I was in Russia once for two weeks and I lost twenty pounds. I have no idea what Scandinavian food tastes like and never will, because I don't want to visit any place that's cold. I actually have seen restaurants featuring the cuisine of Thailand, India, Ethiopia, Viet Nam, Korea, Peru, and places like that. Not for me.

I almost forgot Japanese food. I went into one of those Japanese restaurants where the guy chops up the food and fries it in front of you. The guy doing the cooking at my table made some little remark about Pearl Harbor, which I haven't forgiven the Yellow Peril for, so I left and vowed never to eat Japanese food again. Besides, those people brought raw fish to these shores. I don't eat bait.

I want my food simple and I want it Southern. Luckily, I have found a few down-home restaurants in Atlanta and around the South, so I can still get good home-cooked food occasionally.

Once I was watching my Mama prepare her biscuits. She was rolling the dough. I said, "Mama, you make the best biscuits I ever ate. What do you put in to make 'em taste that good?"

She kept rolling and then looked at me and said, "It's the love, son. That makes anything better."

I'll drink a glass of unsweetened tea to that.

It was also my mother who first introduced me to barbecue. I can even remember the first barbecue pork-pig sandwich I ever ate.

Mama had driven us to Newnan in the '48 Chevy on a Saturday for her weekly grocery shopping trip.

Afterward, she drove us to Sprayberry's Barbecue. My life was changed forever.

We parked under the curb service shed. For those who may be too young to know what curb service is all about, it worked like this:

You pulled your car into the parking lot of the restaurant. You blew your horn. A person would respond by coming to your car and taking your order. It would be delivered to you on a tray that attached to the window on the driver's side.

You sat right there in your car and enjoyed your meal. No standing in line. No making your own salad. No going to a fast-food place, driving through the drive-in lane and talking to a machine that asks, "Would you like some French fries with that?" and the fries are frozen in the first place.

I didn't know there was such a thing as beef barbecue until I was nearly grown and met somebody from Texas. Georgia barbecue is pork. They will sell you some barbecued beef in the South, but ordering it is frowned upon, like passing gas in church.

I would never get over my first pork barbecue sandwich at Sprayberry's. Mama ordered it for me sliced, in contrast to chopped. I still prefer sliced. Chopped isn't bad, but sliced is state-of-the-art barbecue as far as I am concerned.

I have continued to eat Sprayberry's barbecue throughout my life. It calls to me at least twice a month, and I get into my car and drive southwest forty miles from Atlanta and gorge myself. I lose all sense of time, space, and reality at Sprayberry's. I always order two sliced pork sandwiches. (One would fill a good-sized elephant.) I also order Sprayberry's marvelous Brunswick stew, served with white bread as God intended (it's in the Bible somewhere), the delicious homemade onion rings, and then I top that off with Sprayberry's magnificent homemade lemon ice-box pie. And after all these years, Sprayberry's continues to offer curb service.

I always order from the curb. After I eat, I can immediately lie down in the backseat for a few minutes before attempting to drive back to Atlanta. Someone who has just eaten at Sprayberry's should not attempt to operate a motorized vehicle until he or she has taken a little rest.

In fact, there is now a bill before the Georgia Legislature making driving under the influence of Sprayberry's barbecue a misdemeanor, as in, "Lewis Grizzard was charged with driving under the influence of Sprayberry's Barbecue. His blood test revealed a 1.3 level of porcine tendencies."

Houston Sprayberry, who founded the restaurant in 1926, died in early 1991. When I first began eating there, the staff was made up of him, his wife, and their two sons. Shortly before he died, a third generation of Sprayberrys were cooking and serving the food.

Houston Sprayberry was a man of few words. At the funeral, the preacher said of him, "He was what he did."

It was Houston Sprayberry who always collected the money at the cash register. A man came in and ate one day and as he paid his bill, he said, "Mr. Sprayberry, I've been eating your barbecue since I was in the Army back in the forties. It's got to be the best in the world. I've talked about it all over the country and there's no telling how many customers I've sent you."

Mr. Sprayberry punched his cash register and replied, "That'll be eleven forty-five."

I became a barbecue expert over the years, thanks to my mother's introduction to it. I have standards by which I judge all barbecue joints. Here are a few:

• The more the people working in a barbecue restaurant look alike, the better the barbecue will be. Family places, like Sprayberry's, tend to be more mindful of quality. There's usually the head of the family in charge of the restaurant, and that individual will see to it that nobody goofs around or gets sloppy. There are very few divorces or problems in a family that cooks and sells barbecue. A family that barbecues together stays together.

• If a barbecue restaurant specializes in anything but barbecue, it's risky. In other words, if you look on a menu in a barbecue restaurant and it also features veal marsala or broiled fish, the barbecue likely will suffer due to neglect.

• The more religous posters there are on the walls, the better the barbecue. Deeply religious people think it's a sin to serve sorry barbecue. My favorite religious poster appeared on a wonderful barbecue place in Atlanta called Harold's. The poster said, "Get Hold of Jesus Before He Gets Hold of You."

• If the floor of a barbecue place is nothing but sawdust, you're in for a taste extravaganza.

• Don't dare eat at a barbecue chain restaurant. Too many bean counters figuring out a way to cut corners.

• Never eat at a barbecue place that appears to be less than five years old. It takes some time to get it right.

• Never eat barbecue in North Carolina. They put cole slaw on barbecue in North Carolina, which is also forbidden in the Bible somewhere: "Thou Shalt Not Eat Barbecue with Cole Slaw on It." North Carolina ignored that directive and God sent them Jesse Helms as punishment.

• The barbecue won't be any good if it is served in a bun with seeds on it. Harold's serves its barbecue sandwiches on white, toasted bread, which enriches the taste of the meat.

• If the restaurant in which you are eating puts English peas in the Brunswick stew, be careful.

• If the word "pig" appears anywhere in the name of the restaurant, you're probably in good shape. Some examples are "Pig 'N Whistle," "Pig Palace," "The Greasy Pig," "The Hungry Pig," "Pig Out's," and "Mr. Pig," and one I made up, "Pig O' My Heart."

• Never order barbecue north of the Mason-Dixon line. They don't understand it up there.

Beer and barbecue sort of go together, too, which is another story about Mama. She enjoyed an occassional cold one. I never saw Mama ripped, or anything like that, but she would drink a beer. Two were usually her limit.

They sold beer on the curb at Sprayberry's. Mama would always order one, a Pabst Blue Ribbon, with her sandwiches. And she would tell the curb boy, "Can you please bring my beer in a brown paper bag?"

We are talking early- to mid-fifties, Baptist-infested Deep South. Mama, as a teacher, certainly didn't want anybody to know of her fondness for the brew.

When her PBR came, she would keep it in the brown bag and put it on the floorboard of the car.

Each time she took a sip, she would lower her head beneath the window level. I thought it amusing. I thought adults could do anything they wanted to. Later I learned more about Baptists.

Mama did allow me a couple of sips off her Sprayberry beers. Not every time we went. On occasion, however, I would beg, "Let me have a taste," and she would give in.

I took to beer right away. During my high school years, I had a few here and there as well. You could bribe a curb boy, especially at Steve Smith's truck stop in Moreland. And down at Lucille's beer joint in Grantville, you actually could sit and enjoy one at the counter. Lucille didn't see or hear very well, so if you had thirty-five cents, you could count on having a beer from Lucille.

I never had a beer at home, however, until I was out of high school. Mama likely knew I was tipping a few during those days, but she never said anything about it. I was careful not to do something stupid like drink a case and try to drive home, or worse, drink a case and start a fight and come home missing teeth.

On visits home from college, however, Mama didn't mind if I had a few sitting in the living room with her and H.B. She no longer drank beer in any volume at that point. Practically everything that went into her mouth caused her indigestion and a sour stomach.

My first marriage took place at the Moreland Methodist Church after my sophomore year at Georgia. I had asked several friends from college to be in the wedding. They would be over at the house after the rehearsal. I knew they would want some beer. I told Mama.

"How much do you think I should get?" she asked.

"At least a couple of cases," I said. "Pabst Blue Ribbon." I got that from Mama, too.

She bought the beer and H.B. iced it down, of all places in Mama's washing machine.

The party started about eight o'clock. H.B. had joined us, and he had a fondness for beer as well. By 9:30, we were running terrribly short.

Mama had gone to the back bedroom, but she must have heard us speaking of the worrisome shortage. She called me to her bed and handed me a twenty-dollar bill for more beer.

"I guess if you're going to get married," she said, "you're old enough to have a few more beers the night before."

There was only one thing Mama ever prepared for me to eat that I absolutely detested. Liver. I didn't like liver. As a matter of fact, I knew I wasn't going to like it even before I tasted it.

"What's this meat?" I asked Mama the first time she served it to me. I knew it wasn't chicken, pork chops, or roast.

"It's liver," Mama said. "Eat it. It's good for you."

That, of course, was my first clue. She had said the same thing when she pried open my mouth and poured milk of magnesia down it.

"I don't want this," I said.

"Why not?"

"It won't taste good."

(Heard this one before from your own mother?) "But how do you know it doesn't taste good until you try it?"

"I'll tell you how I know," I replied. "First, it doesn't look good. Second, it doesn't smell good. Third, you've never given me anything that's supposed to be good for me that tasted good."

"Young man," Mama said, her voice giving away her increasing displeasure with my attitude toward liver, "you're not leaving this table until you try that liver."

I had plans for the rest of my life, so I realized I would, indeed, have to try liver. I cut off a small piece and lifted it to my mouth. I closed my eyes and bit down on it.

I knew then that would be the last liver I ever tasted. I had some mud once when I was three. It tasted better than liver. I ate a piece of chalk in the first grade. It tasted better than liver.

I spit the liver back onto my plate and made a face like Jimmy Swaggart makes when he confesses he has committed sins of the flesh (fooling around with a hooker who's uglier than bowling shoes in a cheap motel room.)

"Okay," I said, "I tasted it and it was just as bad as I thought it would be."

Mama shook her head in disgust. Then she went to the pantry and took down a can of corned beef.

6

Mama warned me often about getting married too young.

"I just hate to see young people get married," she would say. "They've got all the time in the world to get married. But they go and do it young and first thing you know, they've got two screaming children, living in a house trailer, and living day to day."

I got the message early on. Mama, who didn't marry until she was thirty-five, had the same in mind for me.

But I developed a certain fancy for girlpersons early. My first girlfriend was Sally. She was in my first grade class in Columbus. We often shared the same modeling clay, and I gave her half the chocolate rabbit I found at an Easter Egg hunt. That's love.

I moved away, however, and have no idea whatever happened to Sally. Perhaps she became a sculptress or a Playboy bunny.

I got a new girlfriend in the second grade. Elaine was her name. When we got to the third grade, I went on my first official date. Mama drove Elaine and me to the Alamo Theatre in Newnan for a movie date. It was Frank Sinatra in "Young at Heart." I don't know how I remember that, but I do.

I also remember, even at that age, being a little embarrassed because my mother had to drive me on a date.

In the sixth grade, I dumped Elaine for Shirley Ann. That's because a friend of mine said he'd seen Shirley Ann and her mother at the Belk's store in Newnan on Saturday and they'd been shopping for a training bra for Shirley Ann.

I anxiously awaited the next day of school to see if, and how, her appearance had changed. I broke into an immediate cold sweat and my heart began to pound when she walked into the classroom wearing a sweater that featured two small yet distinct points that certainly had not been there the last time she had worn that, or any other, sweater.

I never actually got to touch Shirley Ann's trainees with my hands, but the first time I closed my eyes and drew her close to me for a slow dance, I did feel something pushing into my chest, and I was filled with ecstasy. What I felt, however, turned out to be her nose. Shirley Ann was quite short, even for a seventh grader.

Our love affair grew steadily. I tried to make her aware of my affection in a myriad of ways, not the least of which was changing my dog's name from Duke — in honor of my favorite baseball player, Duke Snider of the Dodgers — to Shirley Ann.

My girlfriend was quite flattered by this, but my dog growled at me everytime I called him after that, as if to say, "Don't call me Shirley Ann, or I'll bite off your toes."

I also bought her popsicles after school — or, because I was not exactly well-off financially at the time, I would buy one popsicle, break it apart, and give her one stick and keep the other. After licking away at a stick of popsicle, Shirley Ann was a vision of loveliness with grape all over her gums and tongue.

As much as I dearly loved her, and as much as she seemed to enjoy my companionship, I could sense our days were numbered when we entered the eighth grade and we both turned thirteen.

When girls turn thirteen, they are suddenly open game for boys in high school. When boys turn thirteen, it means absolutely nothing, except they're too old for Little League and still three years away from obtaining their driver's license.

As long as a girl isn't thirteen yet, it is possible to hold her attention with walks back and forth to school, a little smoochie-woochie on the way home from MYF, an occasional movie where your mother drops you off and then picks you up again, and popsicle-sharing and dog-renaming in her honor.

Afterwards, however, girls turn their attention away from such timid activities and begin to think about all the possibilities a boy old enough to drive an automobile could provide them.

From thirteen until sixteen is probably the toughest period of a male's life. He is certainly old enough to want to graduate from what few romantic opportunities the preteen years provide, but he is not yet old enough to do anything about it. It isn't really true that girls mature faster than boys, it's just that they are able to discover the back seat of a 1957 Chevrolet long before boys their same age have the same opportunity.

Willard Haines, who had just turned sixteen and who had been given not a 1957 Chevrolet but a 1948 Ford for his birthday, began to show an increasing amount of interest in Shirley Ann at Sunday School.

Shirley Ann's sweaters were growing more and more interesting with every day that passed, and the pangs of jealousy I had felt when my mother first began dating my stepfather came rushing back with a fierce intensity.

Willard did what every other sixteen year old with his first car was obliged to do. He put taps on the bottom of his shoes, started smoking Luckies and rolled them up in the left sleeve of his T-shirt, hung a pair of foam rubber dice on the rear-view mirror of his car, and installed loud mufflers that sounded like the start of the Darlington 500 every time he cranked his engine. He also developed the ability every new male driver must have in order to compete with his peers—the talent to peel a wheel whenever more than two were gathered to watch him drive away. How could half of a stupid grape popsicle compete with that?

I lost my darling Shirley Ann in the blink of an eye, the beat of a heart, the sudden lurch of a '48 Ford, and the screech of two soon-to-be-worn Armstrong tires.

Many were the nights I would lie in my bed and hear Willard Haines' car roaring down the blacktop road near my house, knowing full well that with the changing of every gear and with the subsequent squalling of his tires, my first love was getting farther and farther away. Willard Haines had my girlfriend, and all I had was a dog who hated me for making him the laughingstock of the canine community.

Well, that's not all I had. I had my mother, of course, and I went to her with my fractured heart.

"Have you tried talking to Shirley Ann and telling her how much you care for her?" my mother asked me, tenderly.

"I even offered to let her have the entire popsicle next time," I said.

"I know how it hurts, son," my mother continued, "but just remember that no matter what happens to you or how much you are hurt, your mother will always love you."

For the first time in my life, I realized there was an occasion now, and there would be occasions in the future, when that wouldn't be enough.

Paula had entered Moreland School when we were in the sixth grade, but I didn't consider her overly attractive. She was a gangly child and had not blossomed as early as the lovely Shirley Ann.

By the time we entered high school, however, a lot had changed. From gangly, Paula went to blonde and willowy, and her sweaters also had changed dramatically.

We went on a church hayride one autumn night when we were both thirteen and I enjoyed my first real kiss on the mouth with her.

Six years later, I decided to marry her.

I was in school at Georgia. Paula was in Atlanta, going to modeling school and working in a bank.

Nothing I had seen on campus had compared with her. Each weekend, I would drive to Atlanta and stay with her in her apartment. I would leave early Monday morning for the sixty-mile trip back to an eight o'clock class.

The driving back and forth had become a

nuisance. Then some yo-yo at the bank, in his thirties, had asked Paula to go on a weekend trip. She didn't accept, but I took it as a threat. If I had Paula with me at all times, something like that couldn't happen.

So I asked her to marry me, and she accepted. We planned a summer wedding after my sophomore year at Georgia. We were both nineteen. Mama was the only hurdle.

I was home for a weekend. My mother was in the kitchen cooking.

"I've got something to tell you," I said.

Mothers know. Somehow, they just know. There was no reason for her to speak. I could see in her face and in her eyes that she was anticipating a momentous, and perhaps dreaded, announcement from me.

She walked to the kitchen table and sat down. Perspiration was running off her forehead from standing over the heat of the stove. I sat across the table from her.

"Paula and I want to get married," I said.

Our eyes were locked together. I thought I read her clearly. She had known this was coming, she was saying to herself. She realized the impatience of youth, but if only they really knew what they were doing, if only there were some way she could tell me, tell us both, that we had so much time yet to go; if only she could make us aware of the dangers and the risk; if only there were something she could say to make us change our minds.

I had dreaded this, and I had already played the scene over in my mind a thousand times.

"You promised me you wouldn't rush into anything like this," she would say.

"I know," I would reply, "but I miss Paula so much, and this turkey asked her to go to Gatlinburg with him, and I just can't wait any longer."

"But what about school?" she would ask.

"I'll finish," would be my answer. "I've got a job, and Paula will get a job, and I'll stay in school."

"She's not pregnant, is she?"

"Of course she's not pregnant. We just love each other very much, and we want to be together."

"You're sure?"

"I'm sure."

"But you're both so young."

"We're nineteen."

"You're making a horrible mistake, son," my mother would continue, beginning to sob. I would feel awful about breaking my promise to her, about disappointing her. I wondered if she would come to the wedding.

The scene, however, was nothing like that at all. My mother and I had both grown out of the protective role she had played in our relationship before. She had given generously, and I had taken, a great deal of independence. We had remained close, but she had not fought against her emptied nest.

As a matter of fact, she had begun to prepare me for life out from under her most comforting wing long before I first took flight. She had allowed me the freedom to make a certain amount of my own decisions. She had, more than anything else, given me her trust. I had abused it at times, but never so much as to cause her to take it away. It was because I knew of that trust, and cherished it so much and appreciated it so much, that I had guarded myself against any intense violation of it. Simply put, the primary reason I never stole a hubcap in my life was because I knew it would have broken my mother's heart.

Now I sat before her, having made the most important decision of my young life, and I had underestimated that precious trust. I had not acknowledged the fact that this woman, my mother, was also my friend, and that her love for me would not allow her to come down hard on me for any decision I made. To have done so would have violated that relationship we had grown to—one of mutual respect, one of understanding. I had no way of knowing it at the time, but to have reached that peak of comfortable interaction with my mother was a monumental happenstance, one that few are ever able to achieve with any other person, much less with a parent.

I sat before her, the result of her raising. She would only bless my decision. The little boy who had bound himself so closely to her, when all around him had seemed so unsettled and temporary, had found himself another attachment. She let him go without the slightest resistance.

We talked about when and where the wedding would take place. We talked about who we would invite. We talked about some old times.

"How did you and Daddy decide to get married?" I asked her.

"I thought he would never ask me," she said.

"Were you happy when he did?"

"I didn't sleep for a week."

"You must have loved each other a lot."

"We did. He was always laughing, and your daddy was a handsome man. He had that black, curly hair."

"Do you ever still miss him?"

"When you really love somebody, it never really goes away, even if they do. You have to learn to accept it."

"I'll never leave Paula."

"Don't, son," said my mother.

Things change. Especially when you're nineteen. No reason to go back into a lot of details.

Three years after our marriage, I told Mama that Paula and I were getting a divorce. I wasn't sure how she would take that news, either.

She surprised me. Maybe because of the fact I had finished college and hadn't wound up with two babies in a trailer.

She asked simply, "Are you sure there's nothing that can be done?"

"No," I said. "I made some mistakes Paula says she can never forgive me for."

"Is there anything I can do?" she asked.

"Put your arms around me," I said. I cried on her shoulder. Regrets.

"I'll squeeze you some fresh orange juice," Mama said. "You'll feel a lot better."

Not a lot better, but a little better. I still had Mama.

I would marry Kay. I would marry Kitty. They both were kind and loving to Mama. I would be with Jo Beth. I took her to Moreland to meet the folks. I had twenty years on her.

I introduced her to Mama as she lay in the living-room bed.

"It's nice to meet you," Mama said. And then she added, "How old are you?"

And then there was Christel. The first time I got married, she was still in her crib. But we had found something to bridge the age gap, and no woman in my life was sweeter to Mama than she was. One of the last pieces of advice Mama gave me was, "Son, Christel sure is a nice girl. Don't you think it's time you settled down and had some children?"

I didn't take the advice, and I currently sleep

alone.

I wrote earlier of the fact it was difficult to find appropriate gifts for Mama. It finally occurred to me after she was gone what would have been the best gift I could ever have given her. A grandchild.

What can I say? It just never happened. It's better that it didn't, of course. I will always have certain emotional scars left by Mama and Daddy's parting. What of a child of my own who had to deal with the same trauma?

Still, I would have liked to have seen Mama with her grandchild. I would have liked to have seen the pride and love in her eyes when I put a baby in her arms as she lay in her pain in that bed. I would have eased some of her suffering. I know that.

To this day, I fantasize about such an occurrence. And I have made a pact with myself.

I'm forty-four. There's still time. And if it ever happens, Christopher will be the boy's name. Christine will be the girl's. And I will tell him or her stories about their grandparents. I'll tell them how brave a man was their grandfather. I will show them his Bronze Star and his Purple Heart I have framed on a wall.

And I will tell them their grandmother was an angel who would have loved and cherished them. And I will take them to her grave and tell them they stand on hallowed ground. Christopher or Christine.

"Your grandmother was a special lady," I will tell them.

And I will see her in them, and there will be peace in that.

I'm forty-four. There's still time.

7

I held my daddy's hand as he died in 1970. I'd never seen anybody die before. It was a peaceful thing. He was in his hospital bed, lying unconscious. First there had been a stroke. Then pneumonia.

He was struggling to breathe. He took a hard-fought breath. Then another. And another. Then he stopped. Seconds passed. Minutes. He simply stopped breathing and that was that.

I would have liked to have been with Mama when she died, too. But they told me she went like Daddy. It was Sunday, October 1, 1989. Two days before her seventy-seventh birthday.

Mama's two sisters, Una and Jessie, and my stepfather, H.B., were with her in the living room of the house where I grew up. On the day she died, Una and Jessie both agreed, Mama laughed more than she had in a long time.

"She was really jolly, Lewis," Una told me. "I couldn't remember the last time I saw her so pert."

They said Mama just went to sleep with the three of them sitting in the room with her. H.B., who'd been by her side for all those years, who'd nursed her and fed her and bathed her, had the keenest sense of her. He noticed she wasn't breathing.

"Call an ambulance," he said to his sisters-in-law. "I think she's going."

The ambulance was there in ten minutes. The attendants rolled her out of the house and into the ambulance parked in the driveway behind H.B.'s Pontiac.

There's some sort of law that requires paramedics to start CPR on such a patient and not stop until a doctor has pronounced the patient dead. Mama was pronounced dead on arrival at the emergency room at Humana Hospital in Newnan.

I was in my bathroom shaving when the call came. It was late afternoon. I had dinner plans with Christel. We were sharing each other's lives at the time.

There had been other calls over the years. Usually, they were something like H.B. saying, "I had to put your Mama in the hospital again. She's having trouble breathing." But Mama always got as well as she could get and she'd go back home until another hospitalization would be necessary.

My cousin Gerrie, Jessie's daughter, lives in Moreland, too. She had driven over to see her mother as Mama was being put into the ambulance.

Christel answered the phone. "It's your cousin," she said as she handed it to me.

Gerrie said, "They've put Christine in the ambulance. I think she's gone." And with that, Gerrie hung up in the midst of the anguish and excitement.

I called back. She answered again.

"Are you sure?" I asked.

"They're driving her to the hospital now," she said.

"Call me back as soon as you hear anything," I said.

I was forty miles away in Atlanta. It would take me an hour to get to Moreland. I didn't want to be in my car driving home, not knowing for certain. H.B. called me from the hospital fifteen minutes later.

"Your Mama didn't make it this time," he said.

I sat down on the side of my bed. Stunned. Empty. My mother had been dying for twenty years. I had said to friends, "Every day she lives is a bonus."

Southerners have set words and phrases for the event of death. I rolled out mine, burned indelibly into me after losing a father, grandparents and uncles and aunts.

"She's better off," I thought to myself. From pulpit after pulpit rising above casket after casket, I'd heard, "She's (He's) in a far better place."

Christel sat down on the bed beside me. I turned my thoughts aloud. "But you're never ready," I said to her. "Doesn't matter how much you think you're prepared for the inevitable, when they go, you're just never ready."

The thing that hit me first, when I walked through the carport door two hours after I'd first gotten the word, was that Mama's bed was already gone. She'd only been dead for two hours, but the bed was no longer there. Just a chair and a table with a lamp on it where my mother had been for ten years.

First it puzzled me. Then it angered me. How dare somebody move that bed this quickly? Two hours and already there's no trace of her tiny universe.

I half-heartedly embraced the mourners— my stepfather, Aunt Una, Aunt Jessie, cousin Gerrie.

"Where's the bed?" I asked H.B.

"I put it in your old bedroom," he answered. "There'll be a lot of people coming in, so I had to make room."

It made sense. But as I sat on the couch looking toward where Mama had spent the last years of her life, the void left by losing her felt even greater. Not a trace of her was left in the room.

I was sitting next to Una, Mama's baby sister. Una has some of Mama's features. Their voices were similar, too. She took my hand, squeezed it and said, "She was my best friend."

At that moment, I swear I felt Mama's presence. I felt it in my heart. Never before had I experienced any linkage between the living and the dead. But at that moment, a ray of light shone from behind the curtain. It soothed me. Perhaps some bonds, mother and son in this case, were so strong that even death could not break them completely.

The last time I saw Mama alive, she had said something to me I hadn't paid much attention to. I was standing over her bed. She looked up and asked me, "Son, do you love Jesus?"

"Yes, Mama," I answered. "Why did you ask me that?"

"Because if you don't go to heaven, I'll never see you again."

"You'll see me again before heaven," I said to her in a joking manner. "I'll be back to see you in no time."

She closed her eyes and took a nap. She was still sleeping when I left. She knew. She must have known. And she believed the bond between us could go beyond death. Maybe this moment had been our first contact.

The death rituals in the small-town rural South have undergone very few changes in my lifetime. The only one that hasn't endured is the practice of bringing the body back to the house before moving it to the church for the funeral and burial.

They brought Mama's father, Daddy Bun, back home after he died in 1960. People came in, signed the visitation book, then took their look inside the casket. The phrase most used upon gazing at a corpse was, "Lord, they sure did a good job on him (her), didn't they?" "They" was the funeral home.

I have no idea what changed the practice of a body lying in the home. Perhaps it had to do with too many mourners in too small spaces. Whatever, there was no thought of bringing Mama back home before her funeral.

She had been taken to McKoon Funeral Home after her death. Monday morning, H.B., Aunt Jessie, Aunt Una, her husband, Uncle John, and I would go there to make the final arrangements.

One distinct rite of death that hadn't fallen into history is that of the community making certain the survivors have plenty to eat. I hadn't been home thirty minutes when H.B. said, "If you're hungry, there's plenty of food in the kitchen."

Enough to feed half the state of Georgia, it seemed.

There was fried chicken, vegetables, corn-bread, biscuits, and pies and cakes, from neighbors. A couple of friends of mine from high school days who still lived in Newnan soon came by with a heaping plate of barbecue and a vat of Brunswick stew from Sprayberry's, the Newnan barbecue mecca. Somebody knocked on the door and came in with a roast. Somebody else dropped off a casserole.

I'd been an urbanite for twenty-five years. I had forgotten the love a small town can show at such a time. I was touched by it. I ate some chicken and topped it off with a barbecue sandwich. I recall feeling somewhat guilty for enjoying my food so early into the mourning process. But Mama would have said, "Son, you've still got to eat."

That's what she had said after my dog was run over by a car and I had gone to my room to cry. Mama had come to my bed and said, as she stroked my head, "Dinner's ready."

"I'm not hungry," I sobbed.

"I know it's hard, son," she replied, "but you've still got to eat."

Life goes on and all that.

There are vocal rituals as well, questions that are always asked, statements that are made.

"If y'all need anything, please call me," which means, "There's nothing I can do to help you through this, but it makes me feel better to offer."

And "Do y'all have enough room for every-

body? Me and Doris got an extra bedroom."
Moreland still hadn't got used to the fact there
was a Holiday Inn a few miles north where the
interstate came through. Arrangements were
made for incoming relatives to stay with family
friends.

I drove back to Atlanta late Sunday evening.
H.B. thought it was senseless. "Why don't you
just stay here?" he had asked.

But I resisted. I didn't think I could sleep in
that house that night. There were too many
memories and too many regrets. I would be
safer from them in my own home.

And there were no more decisions that
needed to be made at that hour. The funeral
would be Tuesday afternoon at the Moreland
Methodist Church. Mama would be buried in
the family plot in the Methodist cemetery. The
local Methodist minister, who had taken great
care to visit Mama both at home and at least
once in each of her many hospitalizations,
would officiate.

Another minister, whom Mama had grown
up with and who had also given her much
comfort in her sickness, would also speak.
And H.B. asked me, "Is there anything you'd
like to say?"

"No," I had answered him. I tried a eulogy at
a friend's funeral once. I had choked on my
own words. I didn't want that experience again.

Vodka helped me get some rest Sunday

night. But Monday morning came anyway. My first thought upon awakening was, Could it have been a dream? But a heart beat or two later, reality came in all of its jolting starkness. The first full day in my life without my mother began with a momentary denial. I suppose that's normal. But more reality awaited. The mourning, the comforting, the dream-like state of initial shock must give way to the business end of dying.

Christel and I met H.B., my aunts and my Uncle John at the funeral home Monday morning. A man said to us, "If you need to talk a few things over, you can have the room to the left."

We went inside the room. The man from the funeral home closed the door.

I said, "I want you all to know that I'm paying for all the costs. It's something I had always planned to do."

"Well," said my Aunt Una, "we sure appreciate it."

My family certainly isn't poverty-stricken, but they must rely on the pensions and benefits they acquired before retirements. It was my place to pay. I would have insisted in any instance.

That settled, I said, "This is the last thing we can do for Mama. Let's do it right."

We told the man from the funeral home we were ready. He sat down in a chair in the parlor. "Before we can go any further," he said, "I've got some things I must explain to you. It's federal law."

The man read from a handbook for at least ten minutes. He had to show us all price levels, he said. There could be no hidden charges, he said. We should ask any questions that came to mind, he said. What he was really saying is that funeral homes make a lot of money on mourners determined to give their beloved the best, more as a balm for themselves than anything else. And in that state, they could be led in any direction by the funeral home. Sometimes the government does smart things.

When the man stopped reading, Una said, "We've picked out a blue gown for Christine," indicating, I suppose, that we were shopping with color coordination involved.

We were led to the room with the caskets. I was slightly spooked. We saw the brass. We saw the wood. We heard the price of each. Una found a casket with a light blue lining. Silk, I think the man said. But Jessie and H.B. didn't like it.

"It just doesn't look like Christine," Jessie said. We looked some more. The figure came mostly in fours.

I saw the casket first. The others were looking elsewhere and I saw this casket. It was shining metallic gray. The lining was blue. A heavier shade than the first we saw.

It was the inside of the casket lid that marked it as, well, distinctive. Against the same blue as the casket lining were what appeared to be four seagulls. Three of the seagulls were flying one way in formation. But a fourth had turned away from the others. There was writing underneath the birds. The words said, "Going Home."

Not this casket. They wouldn't pick this casket, would they? Isn't it a little tacky? Would Mama want to buried in a casket with a message on it?

Una saw it next. She walked over next to me and said, "This is really close to the blue in Christine's gown." She called the others over. I stood back out of the way. I had told them it was their decision to make and I meant it. But seagulls?

"What do you think, Lewis?" Aunt Jessie asked me.

"Do you like the birds?" I asked her.

"Not particularly," she answered, "but I do like the blue."

I knew then we would send Mama to rest in that casket. There were her relatives standing in formation before the casket, and she was going away. Going home. I looked at the birds again. I never gave them another thought.

Next we had to pick out a vault. The man said "waterproof" a lot, and one vault was guaranteed to protect the casket inside it for fifty years. It was more expensive than the one with the twenty-five-year-guarantee. I thought, "How in hell would we know if the thing doesn't stand up to its guarantee?"

We took the fifty-year vault.

Then the man said I needed to give him a check for a hundred dollars to pay the man who dug the graves. The total cost of the funeral was four figures, as I had expected. We left the funeral home and went back to Moreland.

The flowers began coming in. Even friends I considered as casual had sent flowers. One of my ex-wives, my childhood sweetheart from Moreland, sent flowers. There were flowers from people I'd never heard of.

And food was still pouring in. The house was crowded with family. I had to ask what child belonged to which adult. There were second and third cousins coming in and out of the house, slamming the door to the carport behind them. Plenty of time for them to know the solemn nature of death, I thought.

I saw my mother's body that evening. The man at the funeral home led the family into the room where she lay. I thought of that old gospel song that went, "Mama's Not Gone, She's Just A-Sleepin'."

Una said, "They sure did a good job on her, didn't they?" There was specific mention of her hair. The man from the funeral home said, "The only thing we had trouble with was her lips. We couldn't get them perfectly matched." I looked at my mother's lips. They seemed perfectly matched to me.

There she was. In the blue gown. In the blue lining of the casket. With the birds. The stillness of the dead amongst the living is always so pronounced.

Dead. Mama.

I leaned over the casket and kissed her forehead, as I always did when I greeted her or said goodbye. The coldness against my lips stunned me. I cried for the first time. Why hadn't I cried before, I wondered to myself. Because there had been no physical manifestation that Mama was gone. Now, I had it. There she was.

We buried Mama on her seventy-seventh birthday, October 3, 1989. The women of the church served us our lunch in the old Sunday School room where I rarely missed a Sunday for the ten years I lived in Moreland.

Then we drove back to Newnan and the funeral home. The drill is specific. The friends gather, too. They look in the casket a last time and give out their condolences. Mama's preacher friend from childhood said to my aunts, "She's better off." He said it again. "She's better off."

Then the visitors are asked to leave the room

to the family. The funeral director ushers everyone out and says to the family, "There's a few minutes left until we leave for the church. This is your time."

I don't remember who was in the room besides H.B., my aunts, and Uncle John, and dear Christel, who had always been so kind to Mama. Even when she was mad at me. Maybe there was a cousin or two. A few minutes were left. Then the casket would be closed. It would not be opened at the church.

We all cried. We all hugged. We wound up in a semi-circle next to the casket. I had one last thing to say.

"If it weren't for Mama . . . If it hadn't been for her saving every dollar to give me an education . . . If she hadn't shown me the necessity of an education and hadn't instilled in me a thirst for knowledge, I have no idea what would have become of me. But she did all that, and I have known success beyond my wildest dreams because of it. I want to put something in the casket that was a direct result of Mama's guidance."

I had brought with me a hardcover copy of my first book, *Kathy Sue Loudermilk, I Love You.* I had dedicated it to Mama and H.B. It was a collection of columns. Several were about her.

I walked to the casket and put the book near her right arm. I looked at her again, for the last time. I kissed her forehead again, for the last time. H.B. walked over next to me. I put an arm around him. He was crying.

Suddenly I felt terribly selfish. My thoughts had all been about me. MY memories. MY regrets. MY loss. But I had lived with my mother only seventeen years. He had been with her for over thirty. His life's mate was gone. That big man's heart was breaking. I said something to him I'd never said before. I said, "I love you."

He nodded and continued to stare down into the casket. I walked away with the others. He should be the last to say goodbye.

It's six miles from Newnan to Moreland. As the procession left the funeral home and entered the town square in Newnan, there was no traffic. The police department had sealed off the road and turned off the traffic lights so we could pass without having to stop.

The officers watching as we passed had taken off their hats and were holding them over their hearts. As we left town and drove down the highway toward Moreland, each car we met pulled off to the side of the road, a show of respect I had forgotten existed.

The little church couldn't hold all the people. As many as had found seats inside had to wait on the outside. I was astounded at the number of people who knew my mother only through my conversations and writings but came to honor her with their presence.

H.B. sat at the end of the right front pew of the church. Christel sat next to him. I sat next to her.

And, yes, I had decided there was something I wanted to say. Only I couldn't say it myself. I wouldn't have gotten through the first sentence. But I had typed my thoughts on a piece of paper and asked Stanley Cauthen, my cousin Mary Ann's husband, to stand and read it. I had known Stanley since our childhoods. Stanley had been my Senior Patrol Leader in the Boy Scouts. I had never lost the respect I had for him for achieving such a lofty position.

H.B. and I had decided on two songs we wanted one of the church ladies to sing. He picked "Precious Memories." I picked "It Is No Secret." Mama had always like that song.

The lady sang the songs. The two preachers spoke. There was mention of Mama's suffering. The Moreland minister said he'd never known anyone to fight so hard in order to continue living in pain. The other minister said, "I've known Christine all my life. There's never been a more loving, caring person. Heaven has welcomed her with open arms."

Then it was Stanley's turn. He walked to the pulpit and stood Scout-like erect behind it. He then read my words:

I asked Stanley to stand in for me because I wasn't sure I could get through it myself. Emotions run unbridled at times like these, and I want this message to get through. Attempting to choke back tears of love and even regret is no way to communicate such thoughts as I have today.

As much as I appreciate the comforting words of the ministers and the promise of eternity afforded by the scriptures, I wanted this eulogy to be read because at too many such occasions not enough is said about the life and times of the one to whom we are saying goodbye.

My mother lived a very difficult life. It seemed every time something went right it was followed by something that went terribly wrong.

She met her love and married him and then had to send him off to war not knowing if she would ever see him alive again. But he did return safely and their reunion produced a child. And there were some happy years that followed.

But then she had to send her man off to war again. He came back changed and broken, and she lost him forever.

Imagine my mother's predicament; she would have been content to have continued as wife and mother, for those were simpler times. But suddenly she was faced with supporting herself and her child in a world that had not yet seen fit to give women easy access to financial security.

But her determination overcame all obstacles. I remember so well the summers she spent at West Georgia College attempting to gain her certificate to teach. Then there were years of night school. This was a woman already in her forties. I remember distinctly the first year she taught in the Coweta County School System; she was paid $120 a month.

And then she met my stepfather, H.B., and they were married. They built a house and order was restored to her life. How I wish that would have been the end of her troubles, but we know it certainly wasn't.

My mother was ravaged by disease the last twenty-five years of her life. I don't remember the last time I saw her standing. We are saying today, "She's better off now." With all my heart, I hope so, because her suffering was long and hard.

But let us also remember this about my mother as well. She was an inspiration to so many. She had a wonderful sense of humor, even through the bad times, and her laugh was infectious. I can remember a time when there was a twinkle in her eye, a lilt in her voice and a spring in her step. That is a favorite memory.

Practically every value I have, she instilled in me. It was her love of the language and her guardianship of the grammar while I grew up that had a great deal to do with my choosing the profession I did.

And how many children did she introduce to first grade? And how many of them had better lives for it?

We all admired her courage. She fought a fight with such tenacity, we should all think of her when the little problems of life get to us. Compared to her, most of us will never know the real definition of pain.

Personally, I would like to thank the Moreland Community for the love it showed my mother during her illness. "Miss Christine" was special, and you all seem to know it.

I would like to thank my stepfather, H.B. I lived with my mother for seven-

teen years. He lived with her for over
thirty, and he was there. Always! A
rock. His loss is the greatest of all. We
lost a friend, and aunt, a sister, a
cousin, and a mother. He lost his life's
companion. Remember him in your
prayers, too.

Goodbye, Mama. And Happy Birthday.

I had been fine throughout the rest of the
service. In the middle of Stanley's reading, I
broke down and sobbed. Christel held me.

We put Mama next to her mother and father
in the plot where her younger brother, Dorsey,
was buried. Each headstone was etched with
the name that the dead had been called by the
rest of the family.

My grandmother was "Mama Willie." My
grandfather was "Daddy Bun." Uncle Dorsey's
children called him "Pop." We had decided to
put "Miss Christine" on Mama's headstone.
That's what her legion of first graders called
her.

It was over so quickly at the grave site. A few
words. Another prayer. Then the funeral people
ushered the family away. To spare them from
the covering of the grave, I suppose.

I greeted friends. My first ex-wife came up to
me. We embraced. I recalled the feel of her in

an instant.

We went back to the house. I told Una and Jessie to keep an eye on H.B. "This is going to be a rough night for him," I said. "The first night alone without her."

I wasn't planning to stay that night, either. Home was where Mama was, and she wasn't there anymore. I said my goodbyes. Christel and I got into my car. I said, "Let's ride over to the cemetery before we start home."

There were still a lot of flowers. The red clay over Mama's grave was moist. A man I didn't know drove up in a truck. He was an older man. He wore overalls.

"I'm the one what dug the grave," he said to me. "I had to figure out a way not to dig up any of your boxwoods in your plot. I just came back to see the pretty flowers."

The grave digger. I was talking to Mama's grave digger, and the man had gone to extra trouble for a family he really didn't know. I thanked him. Only in a small town.

We drove away. Moreland was behind me in a matter of minutes. I began to hum "It Is No Secret."

Christel touched my shoulder. Mama touched my soul.

8

A mother's love is the purest of all. It holds steadfast against any occurrence. It is unconditional. I think of words and phrases from street and song:

— "...a face only a mother could love." I'm ugly, but my Mama thinks I'm beautiful. Or, even Hitler had a mother.

— "The hand that rocks the cradle rules the world." From a country song. Isn't that the truth? What I am is my mother's child. She yet has a part in every decision I make, every step I take. Her influence will go with me to my grave.

— "I turned twenty-one in prison/doing life without parole/but there's only me to blame/'cause Mama tried."—Merle Haggard. Mama tried to tell me, "Son, don't ever have that first cigarette." There's only me to blame.

— "Mama knows...." From another country song. You can't put no shuck (pardon the double negative) on your Mama. She's like Santa Claus. She knows when you've been bad or good. She knows what you're thinking and she knows when you've been drinkin'. There's another country song waiting to be written in that sentence.

— "Mamas, don't let your babies grow up to be cowboys...." — Willie Nelson. That reminds me of another line which I think came from the late Brother Dave Gardner: "Mama said, 'Son, you could make a million dollars as a preacher.' I said, 'I know that, Mama, but what the heck would I spend it on?'"

— "Mama, he's crazy...." — The Judds, mother and daughter country duet. Mama had to quit the act because she's sick. I'm familiar with the drill.

— "Yo' mama." The deepest insult of them all. I was in the eleventh grade. There was a crowd of us, and we'd all been drinking beer.
A boy walked up and I said, "How are you doing, you old son of a bitch?" It's a time-honored phrase. I certainly meant no disrespect. But the boy didn't take it that way.
He said, "Nobody calls my Mama a bitch," and hit me in the stomach.

— "Lord, I Sound Just Like Mama" — a book title. The older you get, the more Mama comes out in you. I did a high school commencement address. I told the kids, "Don't get married until you're thirty-five, and don't ever smoke that first cigarette."

I am my mother's child. And I have one untold story that says it as no other can:

I was fifteen. I was on a boys baseball team that was entering a statewide tournament. The coach said, "You've all got to have a physical that says you're okay to play."

No problem.

Mama said, "There's a new doctor in Grantville. We'll go see him."

Grantville was four miles south of Moreland and twice its size. Grantville had a stop light, a swimming pool and six hundred residents.

The doctor, whose name escapes me, had set up his first practice. I'd had a physical before. I used to worry that I had leukemia. Mama had said, "A little boy in Hogansville went to the doctor and they found out he had leukemia. He died." I also worried about the genital check.

I went to Boy Scout camp when I was nine. You had to get a physical first. An older boy said, "The doctor's going to check your balls."

"Check my balls?" I asked. "Why?"

"To see if they're okay," he explained. "The doctor puts his finger on each of your balls and pushes them up and tells you to cough. If you can't cough, there's something wrong with your balls and you may have to have them cut out."

Cut out my balls? I went into the bathroom and pushed up my balls and coughed. But could I do it for the doctor?

No Camel smoker ever hacked as deeply and as long as I did when the doctor gave me the order.

The doctor in Grantville looked down my throat and into my ears and up my nose and administered the cough test, and I managed to leave there with my balls still intact.

But he also listened to my heart. He walked out of the examining room and asked Mama, "Are you aware that your son has a heart murmur?"

Mama said, "No." I thought to myself, "A what?"

The doctor explained. "A lot of children have heart murmurs. Sometimes, it's nothing, and it goes away with age. But it can mean a valve isn't closing properly."

Now I was thinking, "Can I still play ball?"

The doctor said, "I don't think there's any reason that Lewis can't play ball, but you might want to keep a check on this thing."

Mama had turned white.

"What could have caused this?" she asked the doctor.

"I think it's congenital," he answered. "Or it could be from rheumatic fever. Any history of that?"

Mama said "No" again. Then she told the doctor something I'd never been told myself. "He was six weeks premature."

I was premature?

"He didn't weigh but just a little over five pounds. Could it have been something I did?"

The doctor assured Mama there was no reason to blame herself. But she would never be certain.

I played in the baseball tournament. I played baseball and basketball in high school with no problems. The doctors continued to say, "It's just a heart murmur. It will probably go away with age."

The summer between my high school graduation and the start of college, I worked for a bank in Atlanta. My second day at work, the bank sent me to a doctor for a physical.

The doctor also okayed my balls, but he asked following my examination, "Have you ever been told of a problem with a valve in your heart?"

"Yes," I said. "I've got a heart murmur that will probably go away with age."

"I don't think so," the doctor replied. "I think you have an aortic insufficiency."

"That's not a heart murmur?" I asked.

"From what I hear," he answered, "it sounds like you may have a bicuspid aortic valve. The healthy valve has three leaflets. But you may have just two."

"What's the problem with that?" I asked.

"When a valve is bicuspid, it means it leaks. When the heart pushes the blood out through the bicuspid valve, if it's bicuspid, some of the blood comes back into the heart. The heart has to work harder in that instance."

What is this man telling me? That I'm going to die?

"The problem is the heart is just like any other muscle," the doctor went on. "If it has to work harder, it can enlarge and fail."

"Fail?"

"Cardiac arrest."

"I could die, then?"

"Well," the doctor went on, "I wouldn't be concerned at your age, but keep having it checked."

"So what happens if I keep having it checked and I start to get older?" I asked.

"They are doing valve replacements now," the doctor said.

"You mean heart surgery?"

"They go in and replace the valve with one that is artificial."

"How do they do that?"

"They make an incision in your chest, saw open the sternum and put in a new valve."

An incision in my chest? Saw through my sternum?

"But at least my balls are okay, aren't they?"

I asked the doctor.

"They're just fine," he said.

I walked out of the doctor's office. I was afraid, especially in my stomach. When I was afraid, I always went to Mama. She had saved me from lightning and thunder and bee stings. From stubbed toes, skinned knees and darkness. From growling dogs and my granddaddy's rooster that was bad to peck.

She would save me now. I went to a pay phone and called her.

"Mama," I said. "I've just been to the doctor. He said I don't have no heart murmur. It's worse than that. It's an aortic insufficiency."

"'I don't have a heart murmur,'" she corrected me. "You do not need to use the 'no.'"

I think she was stalling.

I explained what the doctor had said to me and told her about the possibility of surgery.

"I want you to come home as soon as you can," she said. "We'll get a doctor to look at you here."

Nobody in Moreland trusted anything that had to do with Atlanta. They sold liquor in Atlanta in places where you could dance.

Mama took me to her doctor in Newnan. She was in the early stages of her scleroderma.

"You've never had a problem with shortness of breath or fatigue, have you?" Mama's doctor asked me. "I remember seeing you play ball when you were in high school."

I assured him I wasn't aware of any such symptoms.

"Do you think I'll have to have surgery?"

"It's hard to say," the doctor answered. "Hard to say" meant to me, "Hand me the scalpel, nurse."

The doctor went over my condition with Mama. He said to her basically what the doctor in Atlanta had said to me.

She was quiet on the drive home to Moreland. A couple of miles out of town, she said to me, "Lord, son, I hope I didn't do something wrong when I was carrying you."

Mama's guilt never left her after that day. She would say, "I dropped you once when you were two. I hope that wasn't what caused your heart not to be right."

And she would say, "I was worried when you came prematurely. You know you didn't weight but just over five pounds."

"It's not your fault, Mama," I would say. I wanted to tell her of my perfectly healthy balls, but I decided against it.

Vietnam was raging when I left Georgia in 1968. That's when Mama found a bright side to the fact there was a malfunction in my heart.

"I don't want to see you go to war," she said to me. "Your daddy did enough. Maybe your heart will keep you out of the Army."

It did. A few weeks before leaving school, I went to the campus doctor and asked him to listen to my heart.

He listened. Then he told me to jump up and down a couple of times. I did. He said, "There's no way the Army will take you with an aortic insufficiency."

He wrote my condition on a piece of paper and signed his name. I mailed the piece of paper to the draft board in Newnan.

I previously had been classified 2-S, the prized notice that I was a full-time student and was not draftable.

I received a new notice from the draft board in Newnan a few weeks after mailing in the doctor's report. I had been re-classified as 1-Y, a step above 4-F. I figured I would be called into duty only when the Gooks reached the outskirts of Atlanta.

I've carried some guilt about the fact that I was able to skirt Vietnam. I was no peacenik, no hippie. My daddy had been a soldier. He'd been in two wars. And here I was, physically unable to serve. Daddy died two years later, in 1970. I never told him about my heart, and he never asked me about any military service.

But I've always wondered about myself. I've wondered if Daddy passed along any guts that would have kept me in position in combat, or would I have run? Reaction in combat must be the ultimate gut check. The recent war in the Gulf brought it all back again. What would I have said to a son of my own if I had had to send him to the Gulf?

I thought of only one thing: "You'll do fine, son. You've got your granddaddy's blood."

January, 1982. I was married to Kitty. I went to my doctor for a routine physical. He of course, was aware of my valve problem, and he also had told me of the possibility of surgery one day.

But I was in splendid condition. Kitty was a runner. Sometimes I ran a few miles with her. I had stopped smoking. I had taken up tennis ten years earlier, and it had changed my life. I played every day. Every day. When it was cold or raining, I had access to indoor courts. I was thin and swift. Woe be it to an opponent who would hit to my backhand. My forehand side was weakest, but what opponent would think of such a rarity?

That January day I had a five o'clock singles match scheduled. My doctor's appointment was at two. I never made the match.

After my examination, which included a chest x-ray, my doctor asked me to step into his office. Big trouble. I knew it. I sensed it.

He showed me the chest x-ray that had just been taken. He compared it to a chest x-ray taken a year earlier.

"You can see the heart has begun to enlarge," he said. And then he went on, "Blah, blah, blah, blah, blah...surgery."

"Can I still play tennis?" was my first question.

"Not until the surgery," the doctor answered. "We'll have to see after that."

I walked out his door and headed to my car. That same fear I felt leaving the doctor in Atlanta eighteen years earlier was camped again in my stomach.

"Mama," I said to myself. "Don't let them do this to me."

Mama had saved me from so many previous ill fates, and this was the mother of all ill fates, to steal a phrase from the Gulf war.

But what am I saying? I was a grown man. You can't go running to your mother if you're a grown man.

I told Kitty. She cried. I told friends. They wished me the best.

But I held off telling Mama. She already was so fragile. I would wait until shortly before the surgery so as to spare her as much worry, and guilt, as I could.

I went through three months of testing. Finally my surgery was scheduled for late March. They would replace my valve with a prosthesis, a tissue valve that once belonged to a hog.

I sat there on the couch at Mama's house. I had told H.B. of the impending surgery, and he had agreed that we not tell Mama until as late as possible.

H.B. was in his chair. Mama was in the living room bed by then, frail but still lucid. I went over the whole thing. Mama listened intently.

"Mama," I said, "we've known about this since you took me to Grantville to get my physical so I could play ball. Do you remember that?"

"I remember," she answered.

"Well," I went on, "the time has come to get all that repaired. I'm going to have the surgery next week. I don't want you to worry. The doctors are sure I'll do just fine."

She was crying then.

I got up off the couch and went to her. I kissed her on her forehead.

"I don't want you to worry, Mama," I said.

But the guilt that was still in her came pouring out.

"I tried to be a good Mama to you, son," she said. "I hope I didn't do anything wrong."

Once again, I assured her she hadn't.

Leaving her that day was more difficult than it had ever been before. I could die. My youthful sense of immortality had left long before. I think it happened when Paula left me and took the stereo with her.

So what if I did die? Perhaps I had my most unselfish thought ever, at that point. I worried what it would do to Mama. I wondered how she would be told. I was so proud of her strength against her illness. I wondered if she would give up if she knew she had lost me.

The night before my surgery, a few friends visited me in my hospital room. H.B. had come. He would spend the night at my house and be with Kitty the next day during my surgery.

He walked out of the room and left me alone with my wife.

This, I kept telling myself, was my combat. I would not go screaming and crying. I would take this with a stoicism that would prove my strength.

So there we were. Man and wife. What to say? What to do?

We said very little. Just before she left, Kitty kissed me on my cheek and said, "I love you."

A month after my surgery, Kitty and I split up. I take all the blame. The truth is, I just never seemed to like being married. I think it was because of the options marriage closed.

We remained friends after we divorced. Kitty once said to me, "I knew that night in your hospital room you weren't going to stay married to me. I thought you would say things to me like, 'If I don't make it, I'll meet you on the other side of the moon.'

"You didn't even ask me to hold you before I left. You were being too strong. It should have been the closest moment we'd ever had before or would ever have again. But you seemed preoccupied."

I had never been consciously aware of what was taking place in my soul and mind that night before my surgery. But after what Kitty told me, I went back. I went back to the few moments I lay alone in the darkness of my hospital room, the few moments before the medication took effect and I went off to sleep.

Mama. Absolutely. That had been it.

Friends, a stepfather, and a wife. They were pretenders. I wasn't going to spill my guts to them. They weren't going to see any fear and weakness in me.

I had been almost empty of any emotion, that night. I was totally within myself.

I thought, Why was I like that? Why didn't I tell Kitty I'd meet her on the other side of the moon?

Because. Because I had *wanted my Mama.*

I wanted her to hold my hand through it all. I wanted her there at my side. I wanted to hear, "Don't worry, son. Mama's here."

I wanted my Mama. I wanted her there more than at any other time in my life. Subconsciously, I likely was angry that she wasn't there. Angry at her. Angry at the fates for making it impossible for her to be there.

I had wanted her touch. Her kiss. Her hands in mine. Her hands stroking my head. I had wanted to twirl her hair as I went to sleep.

I was thirty-five years old, but it didn't matter. Don't dying men on a battlefield call to their mothers as they cling to their last moments? I recalled an article I had read in a newspaper about an airplane crash. The cockpit recorder had the last words of the pilot as his plane hurdled toward his death. He had said, "This is it. Ma, I love you."

So I had gone back that night. Back to the most solid piece of security I had ever known. Mama. She had been with me through all previous sicknesses, both of body and soul.

And here was the biggest scare ever, a threat to my life. And I was having to face it without the rock I had leaned on so many times before.

Shortly after I left Mama the day I told her about the surgery, she had to be hospitalized again. They said she was dehydrated, but I wondered if worry might have put her there, too.

A few weeks after my surgery, a cousin, Mary Ann, wrote me a letter. She had been with Mama at the hospital during my surgery.

"Your Mama was worried," Mary Ann wrote. "And she kept saying to me, 'I hope I was a good Mama to my little boy.'"

The last words of the letter said, "Your Mama loves you and she's proud of you."

I had a second heart surgery five years later to replace my first artificial valve that had been ravaged by an infection.

And four years later, my doctors informed

me that a third would be necessary sometime in the future.

Mama was gone by then. So one day, as I was visiting H.B., I told him of the necessity for another operation at some point.

"I hate to bring up anything like this," he said. "But if anything were to happen to you, what do you want done?"

He was asking me about my funeral.

"There's a place next to your Mama in the cemetery lot," he went on. "Is that where you want to go?"

"Yeah," I answered him with complete assurance. "Put me next to Mama."